This Is the Night

SUFFERING, SALVATION, AND THE LITURGIES OF HOLY WEEK

This Is the Night

SUFFERING, SALVATION, AND THE LITURGIES OF HOLY WEEK

James W. Farwell

t&t clark

NEW YORK • LONDON

Copyright © 2005 by James W. Farwell

T & T Clark International
Madison Square Park, 15 East 26th Street, New York, NY 10010

T & T Clark International
The Tower Building, 11 York Road, London SE1 7NX

T & T Clark International is a Continuum imprint.

Cover art: Brown, Ford Maddox (1821–1893). Jesus Washing Peter's Feet. Tate Gallery, London/Art Resource, NY
Cover design: Corey Kent

Library of Congress Cataloging-in-Publication Data

Farwell, James W.
  This is the night : suffering, salvation, and the liturgies of Holy Week / James W. Farwell.
      p. cm.
  Includes bibliographical references and index.
  ISBN 0-567-02750-3 (hardcover) — ISBN 0-567-02760-0 (pbk.)
  1. Holy Week—Liturgy. 2. Paschal triduum—Liturgy. 3. Suffering—Religious aspects—Christianity. 4. Salvation—Christianity. I. Title.
  BV90.F27 2005
  263'.925—dc22

                    2004017573

Printed in the United States of America

05 06 07 08 09 10   10 9 8 7 6 5 4 3 2 1

For

The Rev. George D. Young, Jr.,
who first taught me that *thinking* is a blessing to faith

and

Louise Ryals, my grandmother,
who taught me to love questions more than answers

CONTENTS

PREFACE

I HAVE LOVED the liturgy since I was a child. A lifelong Episcopalian, I understand with the passing years the reasons that contributed to my early experience of the ordered relations of the liturgical action as a pleasant habitation. But more important than these reasons is that liturgy helps me to believe.

I am, by the intellectual and existential bent of my passions, one of those persons who find belief difficult. My capacity to believe is stretched to its limit by my experience. Yet, I do believe, and my belief is strongest when I am engaged in the liturgical action of the Christian assembly. Liturgy's ritual rehearsal of Christian life, the poetry of liturgical movement, its awakening in me—or infusion—of the affections of love and longing for communion with God and my neighbors make me more able to believe as I pray than at any other time. I believe because I pray. In fact, I live in a certain way because I pray. I am painfully aware of my shortcomings and I do not know if I can claim to live a Christian life. Only my family and friends and, ultimately, my enemies can make that judgment. But to the extent that I can lay any claim to the Christian virtues of service and love, justice, compassion and forgiveness, it is because I pray. On good days and bad, on the days I suffer and the days when I am at peace, it is liturgical prayer that sustains me; indeed, it is liturgical prayer that *makes* me.

My sense of liturgy as the heart of the meeting point between my limited capacity for belief and the church's confidence in God was sealed and crowned by my first experience of the Great Vigil of Easter, in 1980, at St. James Episcopal Church, Greenville, South Carolina. Recently recovered in the rites of the western churches, the Great Vigil of Easter was included in the 1979 Episcopal *Book of Common Prayer* along with rites for Maundy Thursday and Good Friday. I distinctly remember my first Great Vigil: the lighting of the Fire in the darkness...the procession illuminated by its light, a flame gentle but sufficient...the longing for a redemption from beyond my own strength stirred by the readings of the Hebrew Scriptures...the solemn initiation of converts into the faith...and the celebration of joy caught up in the remembrance of a death. I could see then, through the veil of my old familiar uncertainty, that somehow all of life was there. It has taken many years of reflection on the Great Vigil and on its companions of paschal ritual—the Maundy Thursday and Good Friday liturgies—to begin to understand what I knew that night in 1980: that true Life is a cruciform life; that it is poured out to others and received from them; and that it miraculously comes to birth right in the midst of suffering, mourning, and death...not only there, but definitely there. Such a life is *saved* from all that threatens to crush and destroy what God has given. This great mystery of salvation, celebrated in the liturgies of the Paschal Triduum and crowning the Christian Holy Week, has haunted and inspired me since, throughout the years of my continuing struggle to believe.

One of the truths I have come to understand is that the paschal liturgies of Holy Week are profoundly significant to a people acutely aware of our suffering. It is frequently said that the twentieth century was a turning point in the scale of human suffering. This is not true: human beings have always suffered, and caused suffering, on a dismally grand public scale and in the hidden rooms of our minds and our homes. What is true, perhaps, is that the twentieth century was marked by a quantum leap in our *technical capacity* to cause suffering—often deliberate but not infrequently as the side effect of good intentions—and what is surely true is that the same century saw an increase in our *awareness* of the scale and ubiquity of human suffering. There have been other holocausts, but none executed with quite the soul-numbing technical efficiency of Dachau or Auschwitz; and none about which we have known so much. Thus, the Holocaust of World War II has become a great dividing line in our understanding of ourselves and a great wound in our conscience. Our moral evaluation of more recent inhumanities—in the Balkans, in Rwanda, in the Sudan—is made according to the compass of the Holocaust. The mass and rapid communication of the twentieth century also spread abroad the news of the human mastery of the atom's power, which was unleashed upon innocents with the purpose of foreshortening the suffering of more innocents. Within a more domestic scope, the "learning curve" of psychology and psychiatry brought into every house-hold a greater knowledge of the meanings of mental illness and, with it, an increased understanding of its pain. The complicated double effects of economic development and the stubborn intractability of human mortal-ity despite all our medical advances also entered increasingly into collec-tive awareness. The list goes on and becomes a litany borne of our awareness of human suffering, some self-inflicted, some an inescapable and tragic constituent of our condition.

The historical and textual recovery and analysis of the liturgies of the early church in the twentieth century was carried on in the shadow of our heightened awareness of human suffering. As liturgists worked to inter-pret the writings of Cyril of Jerusalem and John Chrysostom, as they reconstructed or reappraised the earliest liturgies of Jerusalem and Syria, Rome and Spain, the air around them was filled with a pervasive sense of the danger, suffering, and struggle of human life. Working through and beyond the time of two world wars, a growing factual knowledge of the Holocaust, a more accurate account of the human and social cost of Hiroshima and Nagasaki, and in the shadow of nuclear danger, Christian liturgists were inspired to restore the paschal liturgies because they spoke anew to the human longing for life in the midst of suffering. I believe the recovery of baptism and eucharist as the central liturgies of today's churches was driven by the instinctive recognition of the symbolic power of "Paschal Mystery" that they instantiate, not the other way around as liturgical commentaries sometimes seem to suggest. The full justification of this claim awaits a future book, but I am convinced that the recovery of the paschal liturgies was not due to the simple fact of the discovery of new texts or the fresh analysis of old ones. Ancient liturgical texts are historically interesting but they carry no intrinsic argument for use in a contemporary setting. The liturgies of the Paschal Triduum are compelling because they enact salvation in the midst of suffering: thus, they "spoke" to the leaders of liturgical revision in the last century, and they speak to us still.

What follows is an attempt to reflect on the relationship between suffering and salvation in the liturgies of the Paschal Triduum. The journey will take us through some contemporary continental philosophy and theology, liturgical theology, structural ritual analysis, and reflection on the human condition. Like all theology, it is very personal: it is not only the product of conversation with others but the expression of a personal hope. In conversation, what follows owes no small debt, accumulated over many years, to my teachers—George Young, Jim Edwards, Thomas Talley, Neil Alexander, Don Saliers, Walt Lowe, Rebecca Chopp, and Wendy Farley—and to my friends and colleagues, especially Martha Moore-Keish and Peter Yuichi Clark. As the product of redeeming human relationships, it owes an immeasurable debt to my children, Hannah and Sarah and to my wife, Rita, in whose company I have learned the risks, the consolations, and the beauty of the life intimated in the liturgies of Holy Week. The thoughts expressed here developed in the midst of communion with brothers and sisters with whom I gathered around Word, Font, and Table as a parish priest for thirteen years. In the end, though, it is the very personal expression of one who in his own way suffers and who struggles to believe, but who does so in no small part because the powerful liturgies of Holy Week make it possible.

James Farwell
The General Theological Seminary
Advent, 2004

CHAPTER ONE

Introduction

IN A HUMAN LIFE, suffering is not merely an episode, an event, or a passing psychological state—it is a condition. Whether we suffer at the hands of others, intentionally or unintentionally, or struggle against the inevitable internal obstacles to growth that we inherit from our families of origin, or grieve the loss of those who have died, or live through the pain native to the process of psychosocial development, or bring a child to birth, suffering is as much a feature of human life as is joy, wonder, or satisfaction. The soteriological force—the *saving* force—of Christian faith depends upon its relevance to this fundamental human condition of suffering.

If Christianity is to be any more than an interesting explanatory system for those who enjoy the diversions of metaphysical philosophy, then it must open in us a way to live abundantly in and with our suffering, give us hope, empower us to live with others in their suffering, and discern the difference between the suffering characteristic of human existence and suffering that demands alleviation or resistance. That is, Christianity as a living faith must sustain and heal human persons as we "suffer" the long journey of a life lived through the ebb and flow of pain and joy, struggle and peace—

both in what we bring on ourselves and in what comes to us unbidden. It must also inspire a clear-eyed commitment to address, with neither fear nor judgment, the suffering that arises from the corporate sins of injustice and oppression and the personal sins of the wayward human creature. Christianity must open a way for us to face suffering, not as an anomaly or a momentary obstacle on the way to a place where God will be present to us but as an enduring feature of human life in which God is with us. The practice of Christianity must reveal to us a God who is ultimately concerned for us as creatures who suffer, in all senses of that term. If God cannot redeem us as sufferers, then either we are beyond redeeming, or redemption is an illusion. If God *can* redeem us as sufferers, then the soteriological force of Christian *practice* depends upon its ability to open us to such redemption, and the faithfulness of Christian *soteriology*—the theology of salvation—depends upon its ability to attest to this possibility.

This book is a gesture toward a constructive Christian theology of suffering and salvation animated by the simple conviction that Christian faith *does* deal directly, and not accidentally or incidentally, with human suffering as the primary field of God's redeeming work. Simultaneously, this constructive theology is an exploration of the deep rhythms and instincts of Christian faith and a call to hope. Starting from the conviction that liturgy is soteriology in motion, I will attempt to bring the Christian soteriological concern with suffering into the open by exploring the way in which the saving relation between Christ and the church is enacted in the liturgies of Holy Week, especially those of the three days—the *triduum*—that crown the week: Maundy Thursday, Good Friday, and the Great Vigil of Easter.

The Liturgies of Christian Holy Week

There are several compelling reasons to seek the basic instincts of a Christian soteriology in the ritual action of the Triduum liturgies. First, the Triduum liturgies center on the remembrance and celebration of the culminating events of the life and ministry of Jesus Christ: his passion, death, and resurrection. Christians in most every place and age have taken these events as the key to the whole of the divine relationship with the world. Given this fact, any inquiry in constructive theology does well to reckon with what Christians are doing, seeing, and becoming through the celebration of the Triduum liturgies.

The second reason for centering our study in the Triduum liturgies is to correct the relative inattention to these liturgies in Christian theology, given the ecclesiological sea change signified by their contemporary retrieval in the western churches. They signify the emergence of a church "after Christendom," a church that understands itself as a disciplined practice of values and beliefs that arguably diverge from the prevailing values of western modernity. They signify a renewed commitment to transformation—to a life that emerges from death, to a life that involves death to the old order as the doorway to life in a new reality. They put into motion the theology of Paschal Mystery that beats at the heart of the twentieth-century recovery of baptism and eucharist.

Volumes have been written about the eucharist since Anglicans, Lutherans, Methodists, Presbyterians, Roman Catholics, and others have renewed their eucharistic rites and become serious about completing a revolution that dates to the Reformation: the recovery of eucharist as the *principal* and fully *communal* act of the liturgical assembly on Sunday. In fact, the eucharist is presently enjoying an upsurge of prominence in both theological and philosophical reflection.[1] Baptism has received less theological attention by comparison with eucharist, but baptism has received tremendous practical and pastoral attention as western churches attempt to deepen their understanding of ministry as the province of the whole people of God, not merely the ordained. The renewal of proper liturgies for Holy Week, however, is the most significant retrieval of the twentieth-century liturgical movement, making these important liturgies available to modern churches that had forgotten or corrupted them or, in some cases, never used them at all. By the fourth century, in Jerusalem and in many other regions of the ancient church, the liturgical celebration of the pasch emerged as the center of the Christian year and the heart of the mystery of faith. The paschal liturgies of Holy Week were in many places the natural home of baptism and eucharist. If their still-recent recovery amidst a deepening awareness of the ubiquity and intractability of human suffering brings us again to the heart of the Christian mystery, then reflection upon their practice may have much to teach us about our current place in the world and much hope to grant us in our struggles.

The third reason to explore the Triduum liturgies for a Christian soteriological rendering of suffering is the value of grounding our theology in the place where Christian faith is practiced most intimately *before God*. More precisely, I will not simply be grounding a theology of suffering in the rites but seeking it there.

Treating liturgical practice as the site of theology involves the recognition that liturgy is not merely a reflection of what Christians already believe but rather a privileged site where belief arises. In the liturgical action, the assembly, as Gail Ramshaw observes, is "pried open by prayer": liturgical practices enlarge the sense of self, drawing the members of the assembly into a story larger than their own.[2] Bringing to the liturgy their pain and their joy, their longing for redemption and resistance to it, their desires half-formed and a sense—however dim—of a world in right order, Christians deepen their hope and sharpen their perception of the reign of God for which they hope. More precisely, that hope itself arises through the bodily, gestural, verbal, and symbolic ritual practices of the liturgy. In the liturgical action of the church, the faith is rehearsed bodily, by word and song, silence and movement, before the very One from whom faith flows and toward whom it carries us.

The liturgies of Holy Week are some of the most dramatic and powerful rituals in which the Christian faith is both shaped and reflected *in practice,* and the theological worldview that emerges from them takes shape in the form of certain affections and ways of being in the world. For this reason, and because human suffering has first to do not with conceptual reflection but with the lived experience of the human person in the world, our study of the Triduum liturgies' figuration of suffering and of our response to it will take us close to the link between theology and ethics within the liturgical action.[3]

The fourth reason for studying these liturgies is related to the third: reflection upon their practice involves us in the vigorous and promising field of "liturgical theology." Among others, Alexander Schmemann inspired western Christians to recognize that liturgy is not simply a ritual complement to theology, nor a mere dramatic decoration of faith, but is already a theological exercise.[4] This insight was moved along by Aidan Kavanagh who reflected extensively on the relationship between liturgy and theology, particularly through his interpretation of Prosper of Aquitaine's principle: the law of prayer establishes the law of belief (*ut legem credendi lex statuat supplicandi*). Kavanagh took this principle to mean that the primary theology (*theologia prima*) of the church's liturgy is the seedbed of theology in its more narrow sense of theoretical and experiential reflection on the faith.[5]

More recently, David Fagerberg, Maxwell Johnson, Kevin Irwin, Mary Collins, Joyce Ann Zimmerman, Gordon Lathrop, Don Saliers, Edward Kilmartin, Jill Crainshaw, and many others have challenged or developed the idea of liturgy as theology, from which, or in relation to which, systematic and constructive theology are done. Several taxonomies have been developed to account for the various ways in which the relationship between liturgy and theology can be construed. For example, David Fagerberg identifies "liturgical theology" in primary and secondary forms by distinguishing it from a "theology of worship" and a "theology from worship." A "theology of worship" might best be described as a general account of the nature and purpose of worship from the point of view of

Christian cosmology or anthropology, whose first premise is God's initiative toward the human. Such an account might make passing reference
to particular liturgical rites but would not require close analysis of their
structure or elements. A "theology from worship" understands the liturgy
to be reflective of Christian dogma and offers a more or less systematic
rendering of Christian faith as it is visible in its various refractions within
the liturgical action. "Liturgical theology," however, assumes that *theologia prima* is in the "adjustment" (Kavanagh's term) of the people to their
encounter with God through the liturgical action and is not simply the
reflection of dogma that is first formulated elsewhere. Primary liturgical
theology is the fundamental orientation (and shifts of orientation) of the
people toward God and the world that emerges through the very specific
structure and order of celebrated liturgical rites over time. Secondary
liturgical theology is the attempt to articulate those shifts in constructive
and analytic terms that do not lose sight of the organic and dynamic
quality of their source in the people's ritual prayer.[6]

Other taxonomies of liturgical theology than Fagerberg's are possible.
Some scholars, like Dwight Vogel, use the term "liturgical theology" as a
broad descriptor of several types of inquiry, including reflections on
liturgy as theology, theology of liturgy, liturgy in theology, and more.[7]
The present project can be described as a liturgical theology but will not
fit neatly into any of these categories. From one angle, what follows could
be described as a "theology of liturgy," understood in the subjective gen-
itive sense of that phrase: to the extent that we ponder the meaning of
the "paschal mystery," the fundamental organizing metaphor of the
revised liturgies of the Episcopal Church and others, we will be pondering "liturgy's theology."[8] This sense of a theology of liturgy attends more
closely to the liturgical rites than Fagerberg's sense of a "theology of worship." From another angle, the present project may be viewed as a "theology informed by liturgy" to the extent that we will think with the Holy
Week liturgies about suffering but not be restricted to those liturgies in

developing the theology that emerges.[9] From yet another angle, this project might be viewed as an instance of Fagerberg's secondary liturgical theology, a soteriological reflection that follows very closely the specific content and structure of the rites as they are put into motion by the liturgical assembly.

However one might categorize the present project, this much can be said: this project is not an abstract one, but stays close to the structure and content of Triduum rites in the cultural context of their celebration. This contribution to the larger work of liturgical theology offers the possibility that Prosper of Aquitaine's principle can serve as a methodological principle for constructive theology. Not the least important contribution of this energetic field of liturgical theology is that it brings into theological construction some attention to the body: liturgy is, after all, a bodily exercise, one in which speech and thought are caught up with other elements of a total bodily engagement of a human community with the object of its worship. The present book attempts to bring the liturgies of Holy Week, with all their bodily gestures, more deeply into the conversation among liturgical theologians.

The final and pastoral reason for exploring the soteriological significance of the Holy Week liturgies is that a certain instructive ambiguity exists at the contact point between their celebration and the context in which the people of the liturgical assembly live their lives. Put simply, the liturgies of the Paschal Triduum are the point in Christian ritual practice where the readiness of Christian faith to face human suffering squarely, and to find God working in and through suffering, is simultaneously most in evidence and most easily obscured. On the one hand, as I shall try to show, the liturgies of the Paschal Triduum enact the assembly's participation in the paschal mystery of Christ through a structure in which the resurrection is celebrated not as a moment "after" suffering and separate from it, but as a mystery born in and of suffering. On the other hand, liturgies are not celebrated in a vacuum and these liturgies are no exception: they are celebrated in a cultural-historical context where *the assumptions of modernity can overwhelm the willingness to face suffering honestly.*

It is one of the privileged assumptions of modernity that human beings are involved in a grand story of progress in which, little by little, through the interaction of technology and capital, humanity is growing toward a more perfect future. For all their horror, Auschwitz and the Balkan Wars, terrorist attacks, and the sheer intractability of human mortality and pain have done amazingly little to shatter that assumption for many citizens of the modern world, though the victims of suffering know better. Our enchantment with the myth of progress persists, both in societies that have already made great progress in technology and capital wealth and in those that aspire to it.

The conceptual core of this modern myth is given expression in what Walter Lowe calls the "idealist diamond" of Hegelian philosophy,[10] a kind of narrative in which suffering is reduced to an unfortunate but inevitable moment in the process of growth toward a greater good. Because the liturgies of the Triduum have a dense narrative shape centered around the final hours of the life of Jesus and his triumph over death, they can, if celebrated without care and second-order reflection on their practice, become captive to the great modern myth of progress and degenerate into what Johannes B. Metz calls a "religious [in this case, ritual] paraphrase of the social and political processes of modernity,"[11] dismissing the concreteness of suffering as a conceptual step in a grand myth of progress. Living deeply in this myth, we do not face the truth of our suffering, and so we cannot relieve the suffering that will yield to our intervention nor live creatively with the suffering that will not. Living deeply in this myth, Maundy Thursday and Good Friday, and the ineffable silence of Holy Saturday before God's own participation in human suffering, can become no more than an unpleasant stop on the way to the Easter celebration, giving short shrift to the very reality that is the good news of Easter: God's power and will to transform our lives not after we "get through" suffering, but in the midst of it. Far from being a three-day drama that mimics the modernist sense that suffering is no more than an unhappy but temporary step on the way to triumph, each and every liturgy of the Paschal Triduum is a ritual interweaving of suffering borne and hope celebrated. Taken together—and they belong together, as we shall see—the liturgies of Maundy Thursday, Good Friday, and the Great Vigil of Easter celebrate our participation in the life of One who is risen yet wounded, who stands outside the tomb with the scars still on his body, who ascends to the heavenly throne as the paschal "Lamb that was slaughtered."[12]

The title of this book reflects the truth that these liturgies perform and disclose. "This is the night" is one of the key phrases of the Exsultet ("Rejoice!"), the hymn that has long been sung to bless the paschal candle at the Great Vigil of Easter:

> This is the night, when Christ broke the bonds of death and hell and
> rose
> victorious from the grave....
> Of this night scripture says:
> "This night will be as clear as day:
> it will become my light, my joy."[13]

This is the night that is like day, the dawn of reconciliation, peace, and the forgiveness of sin. Yet, even as we laud the candle, we know it burns in the midst of deep darkness: indeed, this is the night when women struggle for recognition of their humanity, when one person strikes another in hate, when the experience of beauty brings sorrow with the knowledge of its impermanence, when terrorists slaughter thousands, when thousands die daily from hunger, when growing up means letting go, when the parent grieves at the untimely loss of a child. Even as we cry in joy at the imminent dawn, we cry out in the darkness of pain and catastrophe. In both senses, indeed, "this is the night." The liturgies of the Paschal Triduum make room for both senses of our night-habitation and form a people in Christ's own spirit who can respond with compassion and joy to the suffering of a world that still waits for the fullness of light.

The Course of Our Exploration

This book, then, is written to draw out the relevance of Christian soteriology for human suffering, as that soteriology is enacted in the structure of the Triduum liturgies that crown the celebration of Holy Week. It is written to show how in the midst of night, Christians proclaim the light. It is both an exposition of the paschal faith celebrated in those liturgies and a defense against their misconstrual according to the pressures of modernity's enchantment with "progress." There are conceptual and practical dimensions to this task, and we will give attention to both.

In the next chapter, we will reflect on the culture of modernity and, in that context, the theological promise of the Paschal Triduum of Holy Week. In this we shall have help from two figures, one philosophical and one theological: Jean-Francois Lyotard and Johannes B. Metz. Metz's work, in particular, supports the instinct that liturgy is the source of a theology that can resist modernity's flight from the concrete reality of suffering.[14]

In Chapter Three, we will briefly review the history of the Holy Week rites from the early church's single paschal vigil, through the development of that vigil into a series of stational observances and beyond, to the contemporary retrieval of the Triduum liturgies by the churches of the west. Summarizing the historical work that one can find elsewhere in more detail, our greatest interest will be in the structural connections of the rites with one another. We will look to the character of the early rites as a rationale for treating the entire Paschal Triduum, rather than the

Easter liturgy alone, as decisive for the construction of a Christian soteriology in which suffering is given its due regard.

In Chapter Four, we will turn our attention to the structure and content of the contemporary Triduum liturgies, setting them in the broader
context of Holy Week and comparing certain features of the Triduum to
the liturgy of Ash Wednesday. The rites of the Triduum, in all their
detail, will be provided. Our focus will be their construction of the relationship between suffering, salvation, and the identity of the worshiping
church, giving us the core of a paschal soteriology—the soteriology of the
Triduum. Here, we will also begin to look at some related themes, especially that of eucharistic presence as it is relevant to this soteriology.

In taking this approach—an analysis of the structure of the rites and
the content of its elements—I acknowledge two risks. To the extent that
liturgical theology is first the adjustment and change of the assembly's
orientation to God and world over time, an analysis of rites outside of
their performance might fail to do justice to the object of our study. One
can argue that a liturgical theology is not generated simply by the analysis of rites but by an analysis of the full range of discursive/bodily practices in a given rite *as performed*. As Mary Collins puts it, "…the content
of the liturgical books—namely texts and directives for ritual action—
does not exhaust the content of liturgy. Liturgy is above all the particular and actual celebration of a ritual event."[15] I have much sympathy for
this claim. However, this book is not a performance study so I will not
deal with particular ritual events. At the same time, I will not analyze
the rites without reference to the way that they are *often* performed, even
though I am not analyzing the practice of a particular assembly. To ame-
liorate the risk of abstracting the rites from their use, I analyze the rites
as they are often celebrated in the coherent living tradition that I know
well: American Anglicanism. Thus, the focus of this study will be the
rites of the Triduum as they appear in the 1979 *Book of Common Prayer*.
Those who know these rites in performance can test my work against

their experience. The similarity of the structure and content of these rites to revised Lutheran, Roman Catholic, and Reformed liturgies will allow others easily to explore the usefulness of this project for their own traditions.

A second and related risk is that my exploration of rites will be misconstrued as an argument that the liturgy automatically generates its own meaning without reference to what participants bring to their celebration. Graham Hughes levels just this criticism at recent works in liturgical theology.[16] He is concerned with how liturgical meaning-making occurs at the intersection between the Christian tradition and the modern lifeworld and argues that liturgical theology must account for the effect that the meanings of that lifeworld have on those who come to the liturgy. I thoroughly agree. That is why, in due course, I will acknowledge the disposition of the participants, the risk of faith, and the role of grace in the liturgical enactment of theology. It is also why I am concerned with one particular feature of the modern lifeworld in which liturgical participants live: an enchantment with progress that sidesteps the ubiquity and impact of suffering. What Hughes overlooks in his own work is the role of the *specific structure and content* of the rites themselves in liturgical meaning-making. That is the data that constitutes the main focus of my work.

In Chapter Five, we will continue to explore the paschal soteriology of the Triduum in two dimensions—"liturgy as soteriology" and "liturgy and soteriology." In the course of this exploration, we offer a provisional account of suffering consistent with the Triduum, distinguish different kinds of suffering from the perspective of the Triduum, and compare the paschal soteriology of the Triduum to other forms and methods of Christian soteriology. It may be helpful even now to pause briefly and situate the task of that chapter with a word about the discipline of soteriology.

As a discipline, Christian soteriology offers a characterization of the agency of Jesus Christ and of the way in which believers appropriate the benefits of that agency. While this clearly implies some form of *relation* between Christ and the church, few classical or modern soteriologies begin from this relation itself, but are driven by a theory or metaphor of Christ's work or of one or another anthropology, working toward the relation as the result of the (logically) prior accomplishment by God in Christ. In other words, methodologically, soteriologies tend to work from the poles of the relation to the relation itself. A liturgical theology, while not denying the initiative of God as the logical *source* of this saving relation, brings the relational matrix of soteriology to the foreground. To study liturgy is to study the *formation* of the people of God: the focus is on the liturgy itself as the *enactment* of the saving relation between Christ and the church.[17]

Consonant with this approach, I will not approach the Triduum liturgies as a mere dramatization or expression of a saving relation already established. Rather, I will approach the liturgical action as the very mode of the church's participation in the saving agency of Christ. Along the way, the questions that will occupy our attention include: What are the dynamics of liturgy by which its soteriology is put in motion? What is the relationship between the disposition of the participants and the ritual as saving action? How does liturgical formation occur? An answer to these questions will require some attention to technical concepts in liturgics, including the concept of *anamnesis*. In the course of this section, I will explore what I call the "soteriological fusion of identities" between Christ and the liturgical assembly toward which the Holy Week liturgies gradually aim. Far from legitimating modernity's flight from the ubiquity of human suffering, we shall see that the enactment of Christian identity in the primary liturgies of the Christian year constitutes an embodied critique of modernity's flight. That critique is performative, but it has a theoretical shape that can be expressed in a traditional theological form.

After articulating the counter-modern soteriology of the Triduum liturgies in Chapter Five, we will conclude in Chapter Six with a practical critique of the Holy Week liturgies in use, generated by their own structural inclinations. Here, I will make some observations about matters to which the local liturgical assembly should attend in order not to obscure the formative power of the liturgy through practices that work against the rites' own deep structure.

This is the course of our exploration. It is my hope that we will reach the end of that course with a renewed sense of trust in the possibility of human flourishing, a counter-modern theology of suffering that is both reasonable and sensitive, and an excitement about the power of the Holy Week liturgies to sustain the people of God amidst the thin consolations of modernity.

Notes

1. E.g., William T. Cavanaugh, *Torture and Eucharist* (Oxford: Blackwell, 1998); Robert Sokolowski, *Eucharistic Presence: A Study in the Theology of Disclosure* (Washington, D.C.: Catholic University of America, 1994); Jean-Luc Marion, *God Without Being: Hors-Texte*, trans. by Thomas A. Carlson (Chicago: University of Chicago, 1991), esp. ch. 5; Graham Ward, *Cities of God* (London: Routledge, 2000), chs. 3, 4, and 6; Catherine Pickstock, *After Writing: On the Liturgical Consummation of Philosophy* (Oxford: Blackwell, 1998).

2. Gail Ramshaw, "Pried Open by Prayer," in *Liturgy and the Moral Self: Humanity at Full Stretch Before God*, ed. by E. Byron Anderson and Bruce T. Morrill (Collegeville: Liturgical Press, 1998), 169–175.

3. On the role of the liturgy in forming the affections, see Don E. Saliers, *The Soul in Paraphrase*, 2nd ed. (Cleveland: OSL Publications, 1991). A seminal article by Saliers on liturgy and ethics, along with recent reflection by him and by other scholars on this matter, can be found in E. Byron Anderson and Bruce T Morrill, *Liturgy and the Moral Self.*

4. A full exposition of Alexander Schmemann's earlier arguments can be found in his *Introduction to Liturgical Theology*, trans. by Ashleigh E. Moorhouse (Crestwood: St. Vladimir's Seminary, 1986).

5. Aidan Kavanagh, *On Liturgical Theology* (New York: Pueblo, 1984).

6. See David Fagerberg, *What Is Liturgical Theology? A Study in Methodology* (Collegeville: Liturgical Press, 1992).

7. See Dwight W. Vogel, "Liturgical Theology: A Conceptual Geography," in *Primary Sources of Liturgical Theology*, ed. by Dwight W. Vogel (Collegeville: Liturgical Press, 2000), 3–14.

8. Ibid., 8–9. The distinction between the objective and subjective sense of a "theology of liturgy" is indebted to Edward Kilmartin, "Theology as Theology of the Liturgy," in *Primary Sources of Liturgical Theology*, 103.

9. This is the term preferred by the North American Academy of Liturgy's seminar in liturgical theology for the type of inquiry Vogel names "theology in liturgy." See Vogel, *Primary Sources of Liturgical Theology*, 10–11.

10. Walter Lowe, *Theology and Difference: The Wound of Reason* (Bloomington: Indiana University Press, 1993), 23–27.

11. Johannes B. Metz, *Faith in History and Society: Toward a Practical Fundamental Theology*, trans. by David Smith (New York: Seabury, 1980), 97.

12. Revelation 13:8 (New Revised Standard Version).

13. The first line is from the Exsultet in the 1979 American *Book of Common Prayer*. The second is from its English setting in the Roman rite. These western forms are adapted from the seventh-century Exsultet, a developed form of more ancient blessings of the Easter candle.

14. Bruce Morrill was the first to give sustained attention to this dimension of Metz's work. See his *Anamnesis as Dangerous Memory: Political and Liturgical Theology in Dialogue* (Collegeville: Liturgical Press, 2000).

15. Mary Collins, *Worship: Renewal to Practice* (Washington, D.C.: Pastoral Press, 1987), 116. Cf. Alexander Schmemann, *The Eucharist* (Crestwood: St. Vladimir's Press, 1987), 14.

16. Graham Hughes, *Worship as Meaning: A Liturgical Theology for Late Modernity* (Cambridge: Cambridge University, 2003), 222, 225–228.

17. See the classic articulation of this observation by Robert F. Taft, "What Does Liturgy Do? Toward a Soteriology of Liturgical Celebration: Some Theses," *Worship* 66, no. 3 (May 1992): 194–211. See also Vogel, *Primary Sources of Liturgical Theology*, 139–148.

CHAPTER TWO

Suffering, Modernity, and Salvation

Theory and Suffering

Our lives are inscribed in theory. In fact, every scholarly discipline now does its work with the awareness that it is rather impossible to be theory-free. We think about our lives and reflect on our experience in ways that always already involve interpretation and habits of meaning-making, whether unconsciously inherited from our forebears or traditions, learned inductively from our experience, emergent as a continuously developing narrative, or systematically developed through study and thought. These interpretive practices, to the extent that they are relatively organized and coherent and can be articulated, adapted, and criticized, are what I mean by theory. Among scholars of hermeneutics, post-critical philosophers, and theologians a great debate has raged for some years over the degree to which we have any access to reality "outside" of our theoretical constructs and learned patterns of interpretation. Although the extreme oppositions in the debate are sometimes overdrawn and the debate itself sometimes overvalued, the issues at stake are not unimportant. However, it is not necessary to make extreme claims for or against the idea that reality is theory-laden in order to make the modest observation that theory both shapes and reflects our experience and that it is not possible to avoid theoretical reflection upon our lives, even if our lives cannot be reduced to theoretical reflection. We will proceed on the basis of this modest but significant observation.

While *theory* is neutral because it is inescapable, *theories* may be less so. There are *theories* that account for our lives in satisfactory ways and theories that do not. In other words, there are better and worse theories when it comes to accounting for the lived experience of our lives—experience that is shaped by theory but cannot be simply reduced to it. Of course, determining which theories are good and which are bad is an activity that itself involves theoretical critique![1] Here, we simply begin with an educated double-assumption: that although there is no non-theoretical "view from nowhere," we are capable of recognizing and arguing over the adequacy of various theoretical accounts of human experience; and that theories which so thoroughly submerge the phenomenon they render as to dismiss or deface the experience of the phenomenon are *bad theories* that deserve challenge and correction.

This book explores the modernist theory of suffering that reduces suffering to its concept[2] or dismisses it as an anomaly, so that it minimizes the attention and compassion *we instinctively know suffering deserves*. To treat suffering as a conceptual moment in a theory of progress erases a great deal of the human experience, which erasure causes only redoubled pain and suffering. Herein, we counterpose to modernity's rendering of suffering an alternative account—a Christian liturgical-theological account—that does greater justice to the demands of compassion and to suffering's irreducibility to thought. Thus, this book is an exercise in paradox: suffering both *must be spoken of* and also *cannot be spoken of*. Only when one is aware that theoretical reflection on suffering must constantly stand under the judgment of the sufferer's pain can one approach the truth about suffering and our response to it. Thinking about suffering only rings true when it bears witness to what escapes thinking.

One of the notions most current in the modern world is the idea that theory and practice are *opposites*. Ironically, this is itself a theory. Its obfuscation is powerful enough, however, that even the attempt to address modernity's dismissal of suffering in theoretical terms itself risks accusation as a vapid conceptuality that does not touch daily human life. Such is the vortex of modernity that even acts of resistance against its assumptions risk being recaptured in the name of under-writing them! With this difficulty in mind, I begin our exploration of the modernist marginalization of suffering with two concrete, real-life accounts of human catastrophe. My hope is that they not only illustrate the inescapable impact of theory on experience, but set what follows in the context of this witness: neither suffering nor the impact of its mar-ginalization exists on the pages of books, but in the lives of human beings.

• September 2, 1998: Swiss Air flight 111, on the way from New York to Geneva, crashed into the waters off Nova Scotia, killing everyone on board. In the hours that followed, television newscasts followed the tragedy in their usual way: recapitulating the basic details of the event; updating viewers as information became available; and bring-ing on "experts" in various fields who talked about the crash in the absence of specific details. Like all such broadcasts, this one was marked by a relentless revisitation of the possible technical explana-tions for the crash, delivered with an unspoken surprise that our technology could fail us and an unspoken belief that our conceptual mastery of the crash's cause could erase the suffering to which it gave rise, or at least erase any future suffering from a similar catastrophe. The broadcast was at its oddest when newscasters assembled clergy, counselors and social workers and asked them to explain what the family members of passengers and crew would be experiencing as they assembled at the airport to await news of their loved ones. What is it like to suffer the loss of the ones you love? What will those who grieve be feeling and thinking? The exchange was awkward because the answers were obvious. Yet, we do not face these questions. We are caught unaware when normality is breached by suffering. Here, on the flickering screen, was the power of modernity: suffering, normally suppressed, is newsworthy.

- Recently, in the emergency room of a small, regional hospital in Memphis: a thirty-year-old woman with three small children died suddenly and without warning of a pulmonary embolism. I stood beside the bed with her devastated husband and two of his neighbors. Later, as her husband made phone calls, I approached one of these neighbors to offer support. With teeth gritted, body muscles strung tight, and face dry, he offered what he took to be Christian wisdom: "we do not mourn as those without hope." His body belied the meaning of the words. His body said, instead: hope forbids mourning; hope denies suffering; hope grits its teeth and counts the hours until a future consolation. The future will bring triumph over suffering; all else is mere endurance. Some hard comfort, perhaps, but surely more the expression of modernity's fetish with the future mastery of the human situation than with Christian hope.

To these two episodes of accidental death—one caused by the tragic limitations of matter and the other by the insistent and surprising immovability of our mortality—could be added any number of instances in which we inflict suffering upon one another—in the Balkans, in Rwanda, in the Sudan. To these can be added the stultifying impact of racism, sexism, and other effects that arise from the peculiar fear that lurks beneath our attempts to secure ourselves by decimating others. Neither our industrial or capital advances, nor our medical technologies, save us from suffering, yet we find ourselves caught unaware by its unwelcome companionship.

Suffering and Modernity

What is the cultural climate that makes grief itself newsworthy, that makes mourning distasteful, that sidelines any experience of suffering? What makes us capable, as one nation, of largely ignoring the extent of the suffering in another (like Rwanda), so long as our resources for continual economic and material progress are untouched by them?

Critics ranging from the Frankfurt School theorists to postmodernists of many stripes have identified from various perspectives the myth of history as a story of progress, the reduction of social relations to economic exchange, and the shrinkage of rationality to instrumentality as distinctive features of the culture of modernity.[3] Suffering is a category of experience that makes no sense in terms of these modern values. From the point of view of human history as the history of emancipation, suffering is an anomaly. Either it is a momentary interruption in the march toward emancipation, or, if it is the suffering of those who have paid a price for what counts a progress, it is likely invisible. Suffering and mourning (or, for that matter, joy!) are unintelligible from the standpoint of economic value. These human experiences have no value in and of themselves: one cannot place a price on them, buy them or sell them, so they are privatized into irrelevance. As Walter Lowe observes, "In the eyes of modern society, suffering is almost by definition that which is to be rejected and cast out. Painful, undesired, it cannot be enclosed within the system of exchange."[4] The experience of suffering is equally non-valuable to technical reason, which aims primarily at the mastery of nature. For instrumental reasoning, suffering is only the unpleasant reminder that the "project" is not yet complete. Suffering—including, in the broad sense, physical and emotional pain, mourning, psychodynamic struggle, the psychic and physical pain of being oppressed, and so on—is simply a nonsensical category within the *mythos* of modernity.

Of the three modern values enumerated above—progress, the reduction of all value to exchange value, and technical mastery over nature—it may be the myth of progress that is the most powerful of all. The notion that the history of human emancipation is a history of progress in many ways incorporates and undergirds economies of capital that trade in instruments aimed at the eventual "solution" of everything from suffering to inconvenience and boredom. The notion of progress itself, which involves at least the idea of a *telos*, is given easily to a narrative structure that explains where we came from, where we are going, and how. Perhaps, as Walter Lowe suggests, the narrative form of the myth of progress arose from the attempt by the modern mind, after the Enlightenment, to reunite nature and history, infusing the instability of the latter with the supposed sense of order in the former by positing—at some point in the past, or future, or both—just such order. As Lowe explains, "From this it is a small step to a fullblown narrative which proceeds in three parts: the *arche* of a primal unity, an original innocence; the division or fall into disunity and alienation; and the telos...of restoration and reunification."[5] This amounts to what Lowe calls an "idealist diamond" and serves as an implicit theodicy in which suffering is explained as an unfortunate but necessary moment in the process toward a *telos* that is a greater good for having passed through the suffering.[6] This quasi-Hegelian movement from origin, to fall, to new form of being reduces suffering to a step in a conceptual scheme, and the raw edge of the human experience of suffering—and the sufferer—slip into invisibility.

Some social theorists, historians of philosophy, and theologians[7] argue that the narrative structure of the modern myth of "progress,"—the structure of the "idealist diamond" that reduces suffering to a concept—was bequeathed to modernity by Christian faith, whose explanatory narrative of human existence shaped human consciousness in the period prior to the Enlightenment.[8] Once the west was "emancipated" from the coherent Christian *weltanschauung*, the basic moments in that narrative—in the case before us, creation, fall, and redemption—became, in a secular form, the categories by which social theories and philosophies of history would be developed. If this is true, then it is not accidental that the categories of the idealist diamond—unitive *arche*, alienation and a restoration all the greater for having passed through the second stage—and the categories of the Christian narrative—creation, fall, redemption—seem very closely related.

Whether or not the modern notion of a history of emancipation, with its idealist conceptual structure, developed out of the categories of Christian metaphysics or from the attempt to reunite nature and history, the modern myth of progress and the Christian explanatory narrative are close enough in structure to become entangled with one another in the modern mind. To the extent that the modern enchantment with progress can be criticized for making invisible a great deal of the pain and horror of suffering—and those who suffer, as well—Christianity also stands indicted.

Consider the case of the suffering of those whose identities, cultures, or very bodies have been subjugated to others in the course of political or social struggle. Because the modern myth of progress assumes a kind of inevitability to history, its narrative shape becomes assimilated to the story of the victor. Lowe is worth quoting at length:

> ...we must ask whether the three-part life story of innocence, conflict and reconciliation does not have, however unintentionally, the same effect as the victor's story. Doesn't it also tranquilize one's sense that "it could have been otherwise" by accomodating suffering within a quasi-explanatory framework? And might it not also tend to assimilate a certain language of nature, with terms such as "force" and "inevitability," to the proper language of history? But here as

elsewhere, history will not become whatever one wants it to be. History does not consent to its designated role within the projected super-history. That is why I call the diamond "idealist." It is idealist in that, despite its intention, it is ahistorical. The diamond intends to capture history, but history withdraws from it like the tide. One is no longer talking about the reality of history. The framework is left stranded on the shoals of ideology.[9]

Not only the suffering of the vanquished of history, but, I contend, all suffering is lost in the metahistory of human progress that constitutes much of the modernist consciousness. Suffering is not ideology: it is experiential, personal, and painful. Conceptuality structures our experience of suffering (or its repression) but suffering itself is not a concept. So, if modernity fails to attend to this concrete character of human suffering, or actively erases it, and the Christian narrative is structurally similar to, or even funds, the modern myth, then the question arises: Does Christianity, too, erase the reality of the suffering of actual human beings? Is the Christian narrative, too, simply a metahistory "stranded on the shoals of ideology"? Is it simply a religious rendering of the story of the victor?

Entanglement of Christianity and Modernity

Some would suggest that Christianity is just such a narrative. Consider, for example, the philosopher that many identify as the chief prophet of "postmodernism." In an assessment that has long since become common parlance among critics of modernity, Jean-Francois Lyotard identifies the modern condition as one in which every science (in both the narrow sense as well as the broad sense of any genre of knowledge) is underwritten by a "grand narrative" or "metanarrative": "I will use the term modern to designate any science that legitimates itself with reference to a metadiscourse [of self-legitimation]...making an explicit appeal to some grand narrative such as the dialectics of Spirit, the hermeneutics of meaning, the emancipation of the rational or working subject, or the creation of wealth."[10] These grand narratives are marked by the general qualities of narrative which include, among other things, the capacity to situate hearers and speakers within a larger framework that overwrites and prescribes the proper place of those hearers and speakers.[11] In a startling phrase, Lyotard suggests that these narratives have a "lethal function" with regard to the remembrance of the past: "...against all expectations, a collectivity that takes narrative as its key form of competence has no need to remember its past. It finds the raw material for its social bond not only in the meaning of the narratives it recounts, but in the act of reciting them. The narratives' reference may seem to belong to the past, but in reality it is always contemporaneous with the act of recitation."[12]

While Lyotard does not deal explicitly with the problem of suffering, he suggests that the experience of the concrete and the individual is submerged and overwritten by the totalizing power of these metanarratives of legitimation. He describes the moment in which we now find ourselves—the moment of "postmodernity"—as a time of "incredulity toward metanarratives."[13] This incredulity is a positive development for Lyotard, reflected in his conclusion to *The Postmodern Condition*, in which he issues his now famous postmodernist rallying cry: "Let us wage a war on totality; let us be witnesses to the unpresentable; let us activate the differences and save the honor of the name."[14] This call to attend to the individual, concrete, and local character of human experience would seem to apply to concrete individual experience of human suffering which, as much as any other experience, is sublimated into a concept by the forgetful metanarratives of modernity.

Christianity does not escape Lyotard's critique of metanarratives. In his "Apostil on Narratives" (1984), he identifies the "salvation of creatures through the conversion of souls to the Christian narrative of martyred love" as one of the several metanarratives that coalesce in Hegel's "distillation of speculative modernity." The narratives "...look for legitimacy, not in an original founding act, but in a future to be accomplished, that is, in an Idea to be realized. This Idea (of freedom, 'enlightenment,' socialism, etc.) has legitimating value because it is universal. It guides every human reality. It gives modernity its characteristic mode: the *project*, the project Habermas says is still incomplete and must be resumed, renewed."[15] Here, the matter of suffering does arise in Lyotard's writing: the birth of the postmodern incredulity toward metanarratives, says Lyotard, is in such tragic events as Auschwitz, a case in which the "capitalist technoscience" that serves the modern project of emancipation also destroys it. In such a climate, metanarratives, including the Christian one, lose their credibility.[16]

Lyotard intensifies the identification of the Christian narrative and metanarratives of modernity in his "Missive on Universal History" (1984). While making no comment on the genesis of Christianity or its internal meaning, he goes so far as to suggest that "the Christian narrative of the redemption of original sin through love" is simply one mode in which the modern project of emancipation is framed. Among the philosophical, Christian, Hegelian, Marxist, and capitalist versions of emancipation there are differences, but, "...in all of them, the givens arising from events are situated in the course of a history whose end, even if it remains beyond reach, is called universal freedom, the fulfillment of all humanity."[17]

Metanarrative and the Narrative Memory of Suffering

Lyotard is not the only one to identify and criticize the entanglement of the Christian narrative in the modern project. About the time that Lyotard was leveling his criticism at the Christian narrative, Johannes

Metz, the Roman Catholic political theologian, was formulating a similar criticism from within the house of Christian faith. What is significant about Metz in relation to the present project is that, in addition to recognizing the problem of the entanglement of Christianity and modernity, his suggestive work hints at a theological response to this entanglement.

Metz, too, believes that the Christian message has adapted itself to the culture of modernity to such an extent that it has become indistinguishable from the modern *mythos*. Having taken up the tools and categories of the Enlightenment into modern theology, Christianity takes into itself the problems of the Enlightenment as well.[18] This is especially true when it comes to the Enlightenment's theoretical remove from the actual subjects of human history in favor of the autonomous, rational subject of the modern history of emancipation. To the extent that Christian language and thought take up that modern subject, which subject is abstracted from the experience of the suffering subjects of human history in order to serve, instead, as the theoretical principle on which the narrative of progress is centered, Christian thinking becomes no more than "an unnecessary religious paraphrase of modern processes in the world."[19]

Like the critics of the Frankfurt School to whom he is indebted, Metz wants to guard the non-identity between the history of suffering subjects and the history of the ideological subject of the modern history of progress. The posing of a facile *opposition* to theory in favor of "experience" or the like is not the way to accomplish this goal. Metz knows that the world of concrete experience "bears the deep impression of many systems and theories and...can therefore only be experienced and possibly changed in and through these systems and theories."[20] On the other hand, he contends that the sort of Christian theoretical response to modernity offered thus far—the attempt to formulate a soteriology that honors the experience of sufferers by gathering that experience into the Trinitarian history of the suffering God—fails to distinguish adequately between "the negativity of suffering and the negativity of the dialectically mediated concept of suffering."[21]

As a more adequate theoretical response to the problem, Metz calls for a different sort of soteriology: not an "argumentative" one, but a praxis that is memorative and narrative in structure.[22] Such a soteriology would amount to a concrete response to suffering because it would embody the narrated memory of Jesus' suffering—the memory of the passion and resurrection of Jesus Christ—by which are validated other stories of suffering that "escape the system of the history of progress and triumph."[23] This narrated memory of Jesus Christ is a counter-narrative to idealist modern narratives of increasing mastery, control, or emancipation of the subject that fail to make contact with the actual suffering subjects of history. It is a social praxis that opens one to suffering, sorrow, and melancholy—and, again, joy—which are suppressed and sidelined by a society whose theoretical categories of human progress cannot render these elements of human life intelligible.[24]

Metz's call for a narrative, memorative theology in solidarity with the suffering is, famously, both provocative and frustrating, and both of these aspects of his work have been efficiently addressed by others.[25] What is suggestive about his work for my purposes here is his insistence on the embodied or enacted character that such a theology involves, and his intuitive understanding that what the church does liturgically may be at least one place where this embodiment occurs. With regard to the former: while characteristically unspecific about how this might occur, Metz claims that the "Church acts as the public memory of the freedom of Jesus in the systems of our emancipative society. It reminds us of an indebted freedom, God's eschatological history of freedom which is gained in the cross and resurrection of Jesus and which cannot be absorbed into the ideal of man's coming of age that is contained in the middle-class history of the Enlightenment or into the apotheosis of the history of liberation by revolution."[26] But where, or in what way, does the

church act as, or enact, the memory of Jesus Christ? Metz is not a liturgical or sacramental theologian, and certainly makes no outright claims
about liturgical practice as the source of the narrative-memorative theological response to modernity. However, in several cases, in both *Faith in
History and Society* and in *The Emergent Church*, he does refer to the
eucharistic community as in some way exemplary of this narrative memory.[27] In a much more recent work, he offers to the debate on rationality
among European scholars the notion of "anamnetic reason" typical of the
early Christian tradition and "preserved" in the church's worship, allud-
ing particularly to the words of institution that the presider pronounces
over the bread and wine at the eucharistic table: "Do this in remembrance
of me."[28]

In a recent dissertation in which he places liturgical and political theology in dialogue, Bruce Morrill recognizes Metz's liturgical instincts
and points up the way in which the "dangerous memory" of the suffering
of Jesus Christ is preserved in the anamnetic structure of the eucharistic
prayer.[29] But, bearing in mind Lyotard's critique, one must ask: is the
eucharistic practice of the church—which is, after all, centered on a narrative that moves from original unity, to fall, to reconciliation—something different than a legitimation of the modern myth of progress, this
time in ritual form? To put the question from the point of view of the
participants: does the "little Easter" of eucharist on the Lord's day bring
its participants into a relation with concrete suffering—their own and
that of others—different from that of the modern subject's flight from
suffering in the name of progress?

The Eucharist within the Pasch

I believe these questions can be answered in the affirmative. The church
in its eucharist not only refuses to forget the paradigmatic suffering of
Jesus but fosters hope in its active remembrance. But an analysis of the

eucharist alone only partly justifies the differentiation of the Christian narrative from the modernist myth of progress. The natural home of the eucharist is in the Triduum liturgies. An adequate exploration of a truly *Christian* approach to suffering must take into account the relation between Jesus Christ's own suffering and resurrection as the church enters into that relation through its liturgical practice, and the primary ritual enactment of that relationship occurs in the annual celebration of the Paschal Triduum, of which the Lord's day eucharist is a weekly revisitation. The liturgies of Maundy Thursday, Good Friday, and the Great Vigil of Easter constitute the semiotic context in which the full effect and intent of Christian eucharistic practice manifests itself. For this reason, the theological alternative to the modern suppression of suffering that unfolds in the following chapters takes the form of the soteriology enacted in the liturgies of the Paschal Triduum. As such, this project honors the concerns raised by Lyotard and Metz, as well as the hints in Metz's work that the liturgical life of Christians is a critical piece of the Christian response to modernity.

Although the Triduum liturgies flowered at the time of the church's turn to a Constantinian alliance between the Christian church and empire, the theological roots of the Triduum liturgies are in the pre-Constantinian period in the church's life, when ritual participation in the church was a practice of discontinuity with the church's surrounding culture. Given that fact, the early church may have something to teach us in our pursuit of a post-Constantinian theology discontinuous, in its own way, with the assumptions of our cultural situation.[30] The early paschal vigil from which the Triduum developed attended to the passion and resurrection in single, unitive celebration. This very early approach to celebrating the pasch reflects an instinct that the power of God in the resurrection is not celebrated so much as a triumph beyond or after suffering, but as a mystery that emerges by, through, and in suffering. In a later development in certain regions, the Triduum liturgies stretched out the moments of the passion and resurrection into several observances, although, as I shall attempt to demonstrate, the early instinct that resurrection comes not beyond but in and through suffering is preserved through the structural connections among the central liturgies of Holy Week. Though narrative in structure, the principle liturgies of Holy Week unfold in a form very different from a metanarrative in three-part structure.

Against Romanticism

To say that the early church's instinct for the indivisibility of passion and resurrection holds the key to a counter-modern soteriology is not to justify a posture of romantic nostalgia for a "golden age" of pure Christian faith or uncomplicated liturgical authenticity. What characterizes modernity is not its allergy to the reality of human suffering, but the *powerful theoretical expression of that allergy*: even the early church shows an inclination to overwrite the reality of human suffering in the shape of its proclamation, even as its intuitions toward the remembrance of suffering are also in evidence liturgically.

Consider, for example, the well-known multiple endings of the gospel of Mark as a literary trace of the human desire for victorious closure. The earliest ending to the gospel of Mark, with its suggestion that even the resurrection of Christ did not eliminate the full breadth of fear and uncertainty that marked the disciples' experience, is soon recast—probably in the second century—as a story of triumph that replaces the liminal experience of terror and amazement with the confidence of certain victory.[31] In every era, the acknowledgement of the ubiquity of human suffering struggles with the propensity to sublimate or ignore it; this seems to be the nature of the human resistance to the mystery of God's Life found in the midst of death. What the early church's observance of the *pasch* offers us is not a more pure expression of faith that accounts for suffering, but an instinct that we can trace through the pre-Constantinian period and into the flowering of the Triduum in the fourth century, even as the human inclination to flee from suffering also persists.

In this connection, one must say that Lyotard's concern with the entanglement of the Christian narrative and the modern narrative of emancipation-as-progress exhibits little awareness that the entanglement of the two narratives does not have its *origin* in the modern period. That entanglement is bequeathed to modernity by the age-old human inclination to avoid and deny the reality of suffering. Though evident in the pre-Constantinian period, this inclination comes to full expression in the Constantinian alliance between the churches and western societies. Under the terms of that social-religious alliance, Christianity served as the spiritual guardian of a moral and social consensus among western cultures that was honored at least in the breach, if not always in the keeping. Arguably, in the Constantinian era, the church had the upper hand in that alliance, so that moral and social issues were addressed in ways determined by the western theological and philosophical tradition. In the modern period, the relationship is reversed: thus, Metz's observation that Christian theology is simply an "unnecessary religious paraphrase of modern processes in the world."[32] In either case, the church (sometimes forcefully, sometimes inconsequentially) underwrites the assumptions of the culture in which it is situated.

What is remarkable is the fact that, in both the pre-Constantinian and Constantinian periods, despite the human tendency to sideline suffering as transitory, the instinct toward the power of God to be manifest under the conditions of human suffering is evident in the deep structure of the church's paschal liturgy. Although the paschal liturgies did enter a hiatus for a time, it is no accident that these liturgies were revived and developed again in the twentieth century at a time when the obscenity of world wars and the power of mass communication once again made clear the relentless presence of suffering on the landscape of human existence.

If, as Aidan Kavanagh contends, Christian worship is not *words about God*, church, and world, but rather *the enactment of world as God is drawing it into new being in Christ*, [33] then the route to answering Metz's call for a practical rather than argumentative soteriology—one that challenges the powerful theoretical account that modernity gives to an age-old inclination toward suffering's suppression—may best be found in careful attention to the world that emerges in the worship of the Triduum.

Notes

1. See David Tracy, *Plurality and Ambiguity: Hermeneutics, Religoin, Hope* (Chicago: University of Chicago, 1987), 9–10.

2. Johannes B. Metz, *Faith in History and Society: Toward a Practical Fundamental Theology*, trans. by David Smith (New York: Seabury, 1980), 132.

3. My analysis of modernity is generally indebted to the earlier critical theorists of the Frankfurt School. See, e.g., Max Horkheimer and Theodor Adorno, *Dialectic of Enlightenment*, trans. John Cumming (New York: Continuum, 1994). It is well known that Jürgen Habermas, an inheritor of the Frankfurt School thinkers, considers their estimation of modernity pessimistic. Still, his acknowledgment that the Enlightenment is an incomplete revolution signals a recognition that our current cultural situation is problematic. For the differences between his view and the earlier Frankfurt School theorists, as well as his challenge to Jean-Francois Lyotard, on whose work I also rely, see Jürgen Habermas, *The Philosophical Discourse of Modernity: Twelve Lectures* (Cambridge: MIT Press, 1993), esp. chs. 5 and 11.

4. Walter Lowe, *Theology and Difference: The Wound of Reason* (Bloomington: Indiana University Press, 1993), 9.

5. Ibid., 25.

6. Ibid., 25–26.

7. See John Milbank, *Theology and Social Theory: Beyond Secular Reason* (Oxford: Blackwell, 1990), 15ff.

8. While "narrative theology" may be a recent phenomenon in Christian schol-arly circles, the narrative shape of Christian faith is not. Early interpreters of Christian faith related the work of God in Christ as a progression out of the work of God to which testimony was lent by the Hebrew Scriptures. The revelation of God in Christ was understood to lend itself to a narrative hermeneutic. Even the most mystical and metaphorical of interpreters, e.g. Gregory of Nyssa, wove their mystical theologies as an exposition of the *story* or *stories* of God's redemptive work with humanity. Particularly relevant to our concerns, most of the earliest surviving eucharistic prayers themselves "narrrate" the mighty acts of God. See Gregory of Nyssa, *The Life of Moses,* trans. by Abraham J. Malherbe and Everett Ferguson (New York: Paulist Press, 1978); Irenaeus, *Adversus haereses,* in *The Ante-Nicene Fathers,* trans. by Alexander Roberts and James Donaldson (Grand Rapids: Eerdmans, 1987), Book 1, chaps. 9 and 10; R. C. D. Jasper and G. J. Cuming, *Prayers of the Eucharist: Early and Reformed,* 3rd. ed. (New York: Pueblo, 1987).

9. Lowe, *Theology and Difference,* 27.

10. Jean-Francois Lyotard, *The Postmodern Condition: A Report on Knowledge,* trans. by Geoff Bennington and Brian Massumi (Minneapolis: University of Minnesota, 1984), xxiii.

11. Ibid., 21.

12. Ibid., 22.

13. Ibid., xxiv. This incredulity partly arises from our increased understanding of the multivalence of human language. Not only is narrative no longer a privileged form of discourse above others, but all discourse is an agonistic process of adjudica-tion between multiple kinds of discourse at the local level according to constantly shifting criteria. See his later work in *The Differend: Phrases in Dispute,* trans. by Georges Van Den Abbeele (Minneapolis: University of Minnesota, 1988), 136.

14. Lyotard, *Postmodern Condition,* 82.

15. Jean-Francois Lyotard, *The Postmodern Explained,* trans. by Don Barry, et al. (Minneapolis: University of Minnesota Press, 1993), 18.

16. Ibid., 18–19.

17. Ibid., 25. There are subtle, important differences in Lyotard's interpretation of the role Hegel plays in the modern project between the two passages I have cited. These need not detain us, as Lyotard's work serves here as an exemplary case of the criticism of the role of Christianity in the modern project.

18. Metz, *Faith in History and Society,* 27.

19. Ibid., 97.

20. Ibid., 18.

21. Ibid., 132. Metz is thinking principally of Jürgen Moltmann's influential work on this point, although a number of European and Latin American theologians are arguably subject to the same criticism.

22. Ibid., 133.

23. Ibid., 58.

24. Ibid., 57.

25. See, e.g., Rebecca Chopp, *The Praxis of Suffering: An Interpretation of Liberation and Political Theologies* (Maryknoll: Orbis, 1986); J. A. Colombo, *An Essay on Theology and History: Studies in Panenberg, Metz, and the Frankfurt School* (Atlanta: Scholar's Press, 1990); James Matthew Ashley, *Interruptions: Mysticism, Politics, and Theology in the Work of Johann Baptist Metz* (Notre Dame: University of Notre Dame, 1998).

26. Metz, *Faith in History and Society*, 91.

27. See Metz's comments in *Faith in History and Society*, 70; and in *The Emergent Church: The Future of Christianity in a Post-bourgeois World*, trans. by Peter Mann (New York: Crossroad, 1981), 34ff.

28. Metz, "Freedom in Solidarity: The Rescue of Reason," in *Faith and the Future: Essays on Theology, Solidarity, and Modernity*, trans. by John Bowden (Maryknoll: Orbis, 1995), 76–77.

29. Bruce T. Morrill, *Anamnesis as Dangerous Memory: Political and Liturgical Theology in Dialogue* (Collegeville: Liturgical Press, 2000).

30. N. B. Richard Norris, "The Result of the Loss of Baptismal Discipline," in *The Baptismal Mystery and the Catechumenate*, ed. by Michael W. Merriman (New York: Church Hymnal Corp., 1990), 20–35.

31. Mark 16:1ff.

32. Metz, *Faith in History and Society*, 97.

33. Kavanagh, *On Liturgical Theology*, 168.

CHAPTER THREE

Celebrating the Paschal Mystery:
From Early Patterns to Twentieth-Century Recovery

I DO NOT PROPOSE to offer here a detailed treatment of the early development of the liturgies of Holy Week, nor will I weigh in on current debates in historical liturgiology.[1] The development of the eucharistic practice of the early churches into weekly and then annual celebrations of the pasch has been adequately addressed by others to whose work the reader might profitably turn.[2] The history of that development is a fascinating and complex one, with ritual variances conditioned by regional concerns, patterns of communication across geographical settings, and emphases characteristic to eastern or western Christian communities. What emerges across these variances, however, is what I would call an "instinct" in the liturgical practice of the early churches toward the indissoluble connection between the passion and the resurrection of Jesus, rather than the resurrection alone, as the crown of the liturgical year. My purpose in this brief chapter is simply to lift up that instinct as a warrant for a constructive liturgical theology centered in the liturgies of Maundy Thursday, Good Friday, and the Great Vigil of Easter, taken together, rather than in the Easter Vigil alone.[3]

The discourse of the early churches did not include a concern for suffering as it is framed in postmodernist terms, but they did know and struggle both intellectually and existentially with the problem of suffering. The pre-Constantinian churches were suffering churches, moving in and out of persecutions at the whim of various caesars. Their instinct toward the saving unity of the passion and resurrection of Christ must surely have been connected to their sense of hope in the midst of their suffering, and I believe that instinct hints at the direction for a constructive theology concerned with suffering in our own day.

Early Christian Liturgical Development

It seems clear from the documentary evidence that the ritual observance of the earliest Christians involved a daily gathering to celebrate the cultic meal. The Book of Acts connects the daily attendance of Jewish Christians in the Temple to the daily "breaking of the bread" in homes, as well as to daily charity toward the widows centered on the common table.[4] Very quickly, however—probably within a generation of the death of Jesus—the eucharistic ritual developed into a weekly observance. Both Second Testament documents and the early church manual known as the *Didache* refer to the celebration of eucharist on "the Lord's day" or "the first day of the week."[5] The latter designation reflects the way in which the early Christians understood the redemptive experience celebrated in eucharist to have transformed the old order in both actual and promissory fashion: the first day of the week was not only different from the weekly Jewish Sabbath (observed on the last day of the week), but became, symbolically, an "eighth day" of creation in which God was at work anew in the saving mystery of Jesus' death and resurrection.[6]

In addition to the weekly celebration of eucharist, an annual celebration of the passion, death, and resurrection of Christ soon developed. Although the most complete evidence of that practice is found in documents from the early to middle third century, it is reasonable to deduce from that evidence that an annual celebration began much earlier. In fact, the first century saw the soteriological significance of Jesus being articulated in terms of a transformed Passover,[7] and Massey Shepherd believes that elements in the structure of Mark's gospel suggest the observance of a paschal feast by the time of its writing.[8] Certainly, the Quartodeciman controversy on the observance of Easter, which took place in the second century, suggests that an annual paschal celebration had been in observance for some time. Regardless of the precise historical origin of this annual event, what is relevant to the present study is the inalienable connection between passion and resurrection that marks this annual paschal celebration. From this very early stage in liturgical development, Christian ritual life observed and preserved the "indivisible mystery" of the passion and resurrection of Christ as the soteriological center of Christian faith.[9]

The Early Paschal Vigil and the Development of Holy Week

From its earliest incarnation, the annual paschal celebration was a unitive event, marking the "Triduum"—the "three days" of Jesus' betrayal and crucifixion, deathly repose in the tomb, and resurrection "on the third day"—in the form of a night vigil, leading uninterrupted into a celebration of baptism and eucharist on the "Lord's day." According to *The Apostolic Tradition*—an invaluable if fragmentary description of Christian rituals in Rome at the turn of the third century—the night vigil was given to prayer and readings, as well as to the final instruction of the catechumens who were baptized at daybreak.[10] *The Didascalia Apostolorum*, a Syrian document dating to the middle third century, comments on the fasting that should accompany the paschal vigil as an imitation of the absent Bridegroom (cf. Matt 25:1–13) who fasted, prayed, and suffered for the benefit of those he came to save.[11] Thus, Eigo observes, "the faithful were imitating Christ" by staying awake and spending the night in

prayer,[12] as did Christ on the night of his betrayal. The memorial of
Christ's passion and resurrection in the Easter eucharist continued to be
marked by the theme of "vigil," as Christians watched and waited for the
return of the Bridegroom.

Over time, the unitive paschal vigil of the first three centuries began to
develop into a more elaborate, week-long set of observances. The classic
example of this change is in the elaborate liturgies of Holy Week in
fourth-century Jerusalem. In *Egeria's Travels* we have a fairly detailed pic-
ture of Holy Week, which begins on the Sunday before Easter with a
series of liturgies whose core is a successive reading from the gospels
through the events of the final week of Jesus' life.[13] Egeria's account
reflects an emotional shift in the intensity of these liturgies as the community moves into the Thursday evening before Easter,[14] when they
gather in the place where Jesus is thought to have gathered with his disciples for their last supper. This liturgy, which includes readings from the
gospel accounts of Jesus' words at the table, continues through the night
and into the morning with other psalms and anthems appropriate for the
occasion. With brief breaks at certain points, the rites continue throughout the morning as the people move to various places around the city that
are associated with Jesus' final prayers, arrest, and trial before Pilate.[15]

The main rite for Good Friday occurs after a welcome respite for the
people, who have been fasting and processing for some time. At this
point, the people gather at the place where Jesus was crucified and come
forward in procession to kiss the cross, which is presented by the bishop
and his deacons.[16] Then, following the cross into a courtyard between the
place of the cross and the Anastasis, they listen for about three hours to
"the prophecies about what the Lord would suffer, and the Gospels about
what he did suffer."[17] These readings are interspersed with hymns.
Further rites ensue, followed by a vigil through the night by those who
are able. Holy Saturday is devoted to the normal morning and noonday
rites, after which they rest while the Martyrium is being prepared for the

Easter Vigil.[18] That liturgy begins, as described before, with vigil readings, culminating in the baptism of the catechumens and the Easter eucharist.

The "Indivisible Mystery" of the Pasch

From its early development, the annual paschal liturgy connected the suffering of Jesus with his resurrection in a celebration of life coming from death. In other words, Christians understood their entry into salvation to come through baptismal participation in the suffering of Christ, by whose passion suffering was transformed into a doorway to new life. The early Christians "would not have imagined that one would celebrate the passion without the resurrection, nor the resurrection without the passion...."[19] Neither was the movement from the passion to the resurrection a simple progression of "successive actions," in which one is overcome by the other, but a passage from death to life in which both are preserved in the dynamic unity of an "indivisible mystery."[20] Marion Hatchett comments on this indivisible relationship between death and life, suffering and salvation, in the early paschal liturgy:

> In the first centuries the Christian Passover was a unitive feast commemorating both the death and the resurrection of Jesus Christ. Even though the Paschal Vigil was preceded by a fast extending over the Friday and Saturday, there was no sense of separate commemorations of the death and the resurrection. It was a single observance of Christ's victory through death and rising to life again and of the Christian's death and rebirth through baptism.[21]

The close relation between Jesus' passion and resurrection in the sensibility of the early Christians is even reflected in the attempt to translate *pascha*—itself the Greek translation of the Hebrew *pesach*—from

Greek to Latin. The tantalizing ambiguity in the term *pascha* results in its translation variously both as *passio* (suffering) and as *transitus* (passage or movement). To the extent that Jesus' passage into new life occurred through and by his suffering and death, the permanently unstable wordplay of the Latin translation is suggestive of the two moments of the "indivisible mystery" at the core of Christian faith. In the light of the early Christian understanding of the paschal mystery, the historical difficulty in deciding for one translation over the other is eminently appropriate.

The liturgies of Holy Week, as they developed in the fourth century, preserved the sense of that "indivisible mystery," even as the church was becoming more at home in the world. One might argue that the development of Holy Week and the Triduum actually underlined the significance of the passion of Jesus by drawing out certain elements of the early paschal vigil—specifically, Jesus' suffering and death—and lingering over those elements of the mystery in their own liturgical observances. The celebration of the resurrection remained connected to those rites by the "red thread" of the narrative of Jesus' final days, which was reenacted in the bodies of the congregation as they moved through the literal places where the events of those last days were thought to have unfolded. In fact, the breaks between the rites were startlingly few and brief, and the expositions to the people by the bishop or archdeacon at the end of one rite were so oriented in their phrasing toward the resumption of the ritual action at the next gathering, that one follows Egeria's account with a sense that the liturgical action was nearly seamless and continuous from Maundy Thursday through Easter Sunday. Furthermore, the Easter celebration still began with a vigil in which the watching and waiting that characterized the earlier vigil's attention to the suffering, and now absence, of the coming Christ was the predominant mood of the liturgy. Thus, it would seem, the observance of Holy Week in the fourth century continued and even intensified the intrinsic inter-relation between the passion and the resurrection by lifting up each element of the "indivisible mystery."

Loss and Recovery

Over the course of time, the Triduum liturgies picked up other practices or settled into a firm rehearsal of practices already underway in one region or another. The Thursday evening celebration, a eucharist accompanied by a strong sense of its indebtedness to Jesus' supper with the disciples on the night before his betrayal, was rather firmly associated by the seventh century with the ritual of footwashing, as well as the stripping of the altar, which underlined the community's sense of the "abandoned and crucified Lord."[22] Also by this time, the intercessions—the Solemn Collects—which date from the third through fifth centuries, were as firmly associated with Good Friday as Egeria's veneration of the cross, which continued as well. As the age of the sacramentaries gave way to established medieval rites, various forms of Triduum observance continued. However, as deep a heritage as these ritual practices could claim, it was probably inevitable that their very elaborate nature would be associated in the minds of the Reformers with the general state of the Roman liturgy in the west, which they considered to be corrupted by excessive pageantry and ritual accretions that obscured the meaning of the gospel. The complex historical process of liturgical reform is, again, beyond the purpose of this book to rehearse, but the significance to us is that the Triduum liturgies fell on hard times, dropping almost completely from the early English rites that are the forebears of the liturgies we will consider in the next chapter. Their recovered forms in the 1979 *Book of Common Prayer*, to which we will closely attend, are found in a section of "Proper Liturgies for Special Days" which is new to the Anglican prayer book tradition. They are organized in roughly the following fashion:

Maundy Thursday
Entrance rite
Readings
Footwashing (optional, but common)
Eucharist
Stripping of the Altar (optional, but common)

Good Friday
Entrance rite
Readings, including the Passion Gospel
Solemn Collects
Veneration of the Cross (optional, but common)
Communion from the reserved sacrament (optional)

The Great Vigil of Easter
Lighting of the Paschal Fire
Vigil Readings
Baptism
Eucharist

There is a very brief observance for Holy Saturday, also part of the three-day observance. These contemporary rites of the American prayer book are very similar to the renewed rites of the Roman and Lutheran traditions, as well as to Reformed liturgical revisions such as the *Book of Common Worship* of the Presbyterian Church (USA).

The Contemporary Rites

The question to which we now turn is what the observance of Holy Week signifies in our context. Do the contemporary liturgies of Holy Week, performed in a modern context increasingly under indictment, retain the early Christian instinct of the "indivisible mystery" of the suffering, death, and resurrection of Christ or deform that mystery into a reflection of the modernist reduction of suffering to an intermediate step on the path of progress? This question requires us to attend closely to the structure and content of the contemporary rites. This instinct, if it is preserved or even elaborated in these rites, can be the foundation for a theology that resists the modern forgetfulness of suffering and belies Lyotard's reduction of Christian faith to a modern metanarrative. As I will attempt to show, the liturgies of the Paschal Triduum are indeed the performative medium and foundation of such a theology, one in which the imagination of salvation and the remembrance of suffering come together in Christians' doxological solidarity with those who suffer.

Notes

1. For some current issues, see Paul Bradshaw, *The Search for the Origins of Christian Worship*, 2nd ed. (Oxford: Oxford University Press, 2002).

2. Key resources include John W. Tyrer, *Historical Survey of Holy Week: Its Services and Ceremonial* (London: Milford Press, 1932); Francis Eigo, "The Easter Vigil: An Historical, Theological, and Pastoral Study" (Ph.D. diss., Catholic University of America, 1969); Josef A. Jungmann, S.J., *The Early Liturgy: To the Time of Gregory the Great* (Notre Dame: University of Notre Dame Press, 1959); J. D. Crichton, *The Liturgy of Holy Week* (Dublin: Veritas Press, 1983); Kenneth Stevenson, *Jerusalem Revisited: The Liturgical Meaning of Holy Week* (Washington, D.C.: Pastoral Press, 1988); Thomas Talley, *Origins of the Liturgical Year*, 2nd ed. (Collegeville: Liturgical Press, 1991).

3. For an example of the tendency toward the latter way of speaking, see Leonel Mitchell, *Praying Shapes Believing: A Theological Commentary on the Book of Common Prayer* (Minneapolis: Winston Press, 1985). While explaining the liturgical year he observes, "It is in this traditional 'year,' and especially in the celebration of the Good Friday-Easter sequence [note the absence of reference to Maundy Thursday], that the work of our redemption is proclaimed and celebrated"; yet, he goes on to say that the Easter Vigil "was intended to be the clearest and fullest

expression of the meaning of our faith and life...." (7) and that the "Great Vigil is the fullest proclamation of that saving mystery" (68).

4. Acts 2:42–46; 6:1ff. See Eigo, "The Easter Vigil," 10; Massey Shepherd, *The Paschal Liturgy and the Apocalypse* (Richmond: John Knox Press, 1960), 12–13.

5. Acts 20:7; 1 Corinthians 16:2; *Didache* 14.1.

6. See Jungmann, *The Early Liturgy*, 20–21. In addition to the theological significance of this "eighth day" celebration, there may have been a practical necessity for sensitivity to the Jewish calendar during the brief period in which a number of Jewish converts and "God-fearers" became followers of Jesus while continuing their observance of the Jewish sabbath; see Shepherd, *Paschal Liturgy*, 16–17.

7. 1 Corinthians 5: 7–8.

8. Shepherd, *Paschal Liturgy*, 34ff.

9. Jean Gaillard, "Le Mystere Pascal dans le Renouveau Liturgique," in *La Maison-Dieu* 67 (1961): 38, 41.

10. It is unlikely that baptism was *reserved* to Easter at this stage, except perhaps in North Africa and Rome. By the fourth century, the period when the Triduum liturgies developed their classical shape, the practice was more common, although there were other liturgical dates on which baptism was performed. See Paul Bradshaw, "'*Diem baptismo sollemniorum*': Initation and Easter in Christian Antiquity," in *Living Water, Sealing Spirit: Readings on Christian Initiation*, ed. by Maxwell Johnson (Collegeville: Liturgical Press, 1995), 137–147.

11. Hippolytus, *Apostolic Tradition*, trans. by Geoffrey J. Cuming (Bramcote, Notts: Grove Books, 1976), sects. 20–21; *Didascalia Apostolorum*, trans. by R. Hugh Connolly (Oxford: Clarendon, 1929), ch. 21 passim.

12. Eigo, "The Easter Vigil," 35.

13. *Egeria's Travels*, trans. and ed. by John Wilkinson (London: SPCK, 1971).

14. This is reflected in the archdeacon's announcement at the dismissal of the people from the day's earlier rites, which Egeria quotes as follows: "Let us meet tonight at seven o'clock in the church on the Eleona. There is a great effort ahead of us tonight!" (*Egeria's Travels*, 35.1).

15. Ibid., 35.2–36.5.

16. Ibid., 37.1–3.

17. Ibid., 37.5–6.

18. Ibid., 37.8–38.1.

19. Gaillard, "La Mystere Paschal," 38.

20. Ibid., 41: "Paques, ce n'est pas simplement la passion et la resurrection, comme deux actes successifs. Non, Paques est le passage de l'un a l'autre, le mouvement, l'unite dynamique de l'un et l'autre moment de ce mystere indivisible."

21. Marion Hatchett, *Commentary on the American Prayer Book* (New York: Seabury, 1980), 231–232.

22. Stevenson, *Jerusalem Revisited,* 46. Footwashing was considered in some places to be nearly sacramental; this is visible in Ambrose's writings (*On the Sacraments and on the Mysteries,* ed. by J. H. Strawley, trans. by T. Thompson [London: SPCK, 1950], Bk. 3, sects. 4 and 5) in which he reflects on the variant Milanese practice of footwashing at the Easter baptism.

CHAPTER FOUR

The Paschal Soteriology of the Triduum (I):
Structure and Incorporation

GORDON LATHROP'S *Holy Things* is an exquisitely written example of a derived or secondary liturgical theology. In *Holy Things*, Lathrop argues that the meaning of liturgy is a function of its structure, and that the structure of Christian liturgy is a complex pattern of ritual juxtapositions. Particular practices—e.g., bathing, the sharing of a common meal, the observance of a holy day—each *signify* in certain ways when practiced in their original contexts. When two or more such practices are ritually juxtaposed in a new context, the meaning of the new ritual is generated by this juxtaposition of the old elements. Lathrop argues that this way of generating ritual meaning is consistent with the way the biblical texts generate meaning as well:

> Meaning occurs through structure, by one thing set next to another. The scheduling of the *ordo*, the setting of one liturgical thing next to another in the shape of the liturgy, evokes and replicates the deep structure of biblical language, the use of the old to say the new by means of juxtaposition.[1]

Lathrop suggests a number of examples of this operation, including the annual juxtaposition of the fasting, vigil, and meal practices of Passover with preaching and intercessions recalling the death and resurrection of Jesus, and the weekly juxtaposition of the synagogue's synaxis with the communal meal that commemorates Jesus' dying and rising. Christian baptism in the context of eucharist and the communal meal of the "eighth day" set alongside the keeping of the sabbath are other examples.[2] All both destroy and preserve the old by using the old to speak the new.[3]

For Lathrop, this pattern of juxtaposition is no artificial hermeneutic for ritual studies. Reflecting his commitment to the primacy of liturgy for theological construction,[4] Lathrop believes this liturgical pattern lies very close to the heart of the Christian faith:

> It is not just reading and preaching that propose this pattern. So do the sacramental actions. So do the metaphoric chains of liturgical poetry. So does ritual action set next to ritual word. So does singing around the texts. The preaching, when it is thus deeply understood, means only to bring to explicit speech the intention of the whole complex. All the juxtapositions of the liturgy call us to trust in the biblical pattern, reinterpreting our world from and living out of this: God is the one who brings something out of nothing, life out of death, the new out of the old. Thus all the liturgy "invites us into the pattern of these good things."[5]

Lathrop goes on to develop in *Holy Things* an explication of the liturgical *ordo* in substantive terms that possess theoretical and pastoral implications. That work is of great merit, but lies beyond the scope of this study. What Lathrop offers to the present project is a method that can be adapted for the interpretation of the enacted theology of the Triduum liturgies.

Lathrop concerns himself, if I may qualify his terminology, with *longi-*

tudinal or *historical* juxtaposition. That is, he concerns himself with the way in which certain ritual and everyday forms of activity generate new meaning when they are commuted from one context and placed along-side forms from another context. Lathrop's analysis of liturgical juxtaposition provides a fruitful way of thinking about how liturgy does what it does: how, from the liturgical action over time, meaning emerges in patterns that ultimately form a worldview in which the church, and individual believers, locate themselves. This form of juxtaposition is certainly at play in the individual Triduum liturgies: the washing of feet alongside the common meal and scriptural reading on Maundy Thursday; the recounting of the exodus and the prophecies of the Old Testament alongside washing and the meal in the Easter Vigil.

What I shall do in the following pages, however, is primarily an interpretation of the *lateral* juxtaposition of the Triduum liturgies: with regard to the issue that concerns us—human suffering—what is significant is the examination of the three liturgies of the Triduum alongside one another and the holding of all three *in juxtaposition* as the center of the Christian year. This is the approach to which the church's instinct toward the unity of the paschal mystery presses us. This is the approach that yields a full-bodied sense of the Christian gospel. For example, the Maundy Thursday liturgy, by itself, models a life of service and orientation to the other, but this communicates little about the life-giving nature of servanthood unless it is placed alongside the Easter hope. The latter, on the other hand, is evacuated of all but an abstract hope, costing nothing and lacking ethical shape, without its juxtaposition to the liturgy of Good Friday. It is not only the historical juxtaposition of the elements of each liturgy, but the lateral juxtaposition of the three to each other that yields their distinctive soteriology and can answer the criticism of Christian theology as little more than a religious code for modernity.

We turn, then, to an analysis of the contemporary liturgies of the Triduum in lateral juxtaposition with one another. We do so with an eye to the form of life they enact in the body and bodies of the assembly as it relates to the servant ministry of Christ. This is the core of the Triduum's paschal soteriology.

Setting the Scene: The Palm Sunday Liturgy

An analysis of the Triduum liturgies begins with a look at the ritual context in which they are located, because the soteriological import of the Maundy Thursday and Good Friday liturgies are illuminated by their contrast with certain features of earlier liturgies.[6] The Triduum liturgies are the conclusion and center of Holy Week, which begins on Palm Sunday and continues through the week with a number of optional liturgical customs such as the Stations of the Cross and Tenebrae.[7] Holy Week, in turn, occurs in the context of Lent, a period of preparation for the annual celebration of the Paschal Mystery. The importance of the Triduum is underlined by these periods of preparation that developed rather early in the church's life.

The Palm Sunday liturgy (also known, in some traditions, as Passion Sunday), is a eucharistic service of profound honesty: it provides the occasion for the faithful to bring to consciousness the uneasy coexistence between their celebration of Christ's ministry and their reluctance to follow in the same path.[8] The liturgy begins with the following blessing of palms:

> It is right to praise you, Almighty God, for the acts of love by which you have redeemed us through your Son Jesus Christ....On this day he entered the holy city of Jerusalem in triumph, and was proclaimed as King of kings by those who spread their garments and branches of palm along his way. Let these branches be for us signs of his victory, and grant that we who bear them in his name may ever hail him as our King, and follow him in the way that leads to eternal life....[9]

Notice that this blessing includes no explicit reference to the suffering of Christ. In most places where the physical configuration of space allows, the people follow in procession into the church, thus dramatically reenacting Jesus' entry into Jerusalem. This is traditionally accompanied by the anthem or congregational chant, "Blessed is he who comes in the name of the Lord"—an acclamation that also serves as the opening of the service, and which also situates the congregation in the place of the people who witnessed Jesus' entry into Jerusalem. This "Liturgy of the Palms" that begins the Palm Sunday eucharist evokes a mood of celebration and welcome.

This celebratory mood changes very rapidly, however. A pause in the procession allows for a collect in which the celebrant prays:

> Almighty God, whose most dear Son went not up to joy but first he suffered pain, and entered not into glory before he was crucified: Mercifully grant that we, walking in the way of the cross, may find it none other than the way of life and peace....[10]

This is followed very soon, upon arrival in the worship space, with the Collect of the Day:

> Almighty and everliving God, in your tender love for the human race you sent your Son our Savior Jesus Christ to take upon him our nature, to suffer death upon the cross, giving us the example of his great humility: Mercifully grant that we may walk in the way of his suffering, and also share in his resurrection; through Jesus Christ our Lord....[11]

These collects initiate a revolution in the orientation of the congregation. They begin as a body welcoming Jesus, and move very quickly to an acknowledgment of the ultimate end to which his journey will take him. In their petition to "walk in the way of his suffering," they also anticipate a pattern of imitation that carries the soteriological weight of the Triduum liturgies, as we shall see. The revolution is completed by the move into the Liturgy of the Word, in which the congregation is confronted with the full horror of Jesus' end, and with their complicity in it. In many places, the passion gospel is read from a script in which the entire congregation plays a part: when Jesus' trial is recounted, the people assume the role of the crowd around Pilate by shouting, "Crucify him!" The service continues, after the usual elements of homily, prayers, and confession, with the celebration of communion, by which the people receive from the one whom they have both welcomed and repudiated.

The significance of this ritual for our inquiry is that the Palm Sunday liturgy bodily and verbally situates the congregation in the role of receivers, observers, and responders to the action of Jesus. Whether shouting "Hosanna!" in the Liturgy of the Palms, or "Crucify him!" in the Liturgy of the Word, the congregation both celebrates and resists the path of Christ. In either case, they are primarily in a relationship of nonidentity with the person of Jesus. Although the eucharist's sense of intimate communion is also part of this day, the dominant tone of this liturgy situates the participants in an observant orientation. The final chapters of a story of monumental significance have commenced, and they are watching and waiting for the next chapter to unfold. This observer's orientation is critical to note, because this constitutes the beginning point for a major shift that occurs in the Triduum liturgies.

From Observation to Participation: The Maundy Thursday Liturgy

When the congregation gathers for the Maundy Thursday ritual, they come following Palm Sunday's fresh rehearsal of their own ambivalence toward Jesus and with the awareness that his catastrophic suffering is imminent. The Maundy Thursday liturgy itself is occupied by attention to the events leading directly up to Jesus' betrayal and arrest. This usually involves a dual focus on the footwashing recounted in the Johannine gospel, and on the last supper of Jesus with his disciples.

The gathering rite, which begins in the customary way for any eucharist, concludes with a collect that recalls the institution of eucharist by Jesus "on the night before he suffered" and asks that "we may receive it thankfully in remembrance of Jesus Christ our Lord, who in these Holy Mysteries gives us a pledge of eternal life."[12] The first reading, from the twelfth chapter of the Book of Exodus, recounts the institution of the passover. It is followed by Paul's discourse on the eucharist in which he claims "as often as you eat this bread and drink the cup, you proclaim the Lord's death until he comes."[13] Here is a remembrance of the Passover of the Lord in which the slaughter of the Lamb is linked with deliverance from bondage and the anticipation of the fullness of that redemption. These two readings, which set the symbolic context for the eucharist, are followed finally by the reading of the gospel lection, which is normally the Johannine account of Jesus washing the feet of his disciples.[14] This reading sets up the major shift in the Triduum liturgies: no longer observers and responders in a third person relation with Jesus, those gathered for this liturgy are now called to imitate Jesus.[15] That is the "point" that Jesus makes in the footwashing account:

> After he had washed their feet, had put on his robe, and had returned to the table, he said to them, "Do you know what I have done to you? You call me Teacher and Lord—and you are right, for that is what I am. So if I, your Lord and Teacher, have washed your feet, you also ought to wash one another's feet. For I have set you an example, that you also should do as I have done to you."[16]

The form for the footwashing proposed in the *Book of Occasional Services*—a non-binding, supplementary companion to the *Book of Common Prayer*—implies that the footwashing is done for the people by the priest, so that the community's leader performs an act of service parallel to that of Jesus for the community he led. It is a better practice if all participate in the washing of feet—a matter we will consider in Chapter Six—but the theology is clear in the bidding provided by the aforementioned manual:

> Therefore, I invite you who share in the royal priesthood of Christ to come forward, that I may recall whose servant I am by following the example of my Master. But come remembering his admonition that what will be done for you is also to be done by you to others, for "a servant is not greater than his master, nor is the one who is sent greater than the one who sent him. If you know these things, blessed are you if you do them."[17]

After a homily elaborating the themes of these lections, the congregation moves immediately to practice the imitation to which they are called. The footwashing is presented, through accompanying exhortation and hymnody, as an act through which, by washing one another's feet, the congregants take on the servant identity of Jesus who washed the feet of their forebears. In contrast to the Palm Sunday celebration, in which the congregation stood primarily in the place of the crowds by reenacting both their positive and negative responses to Jesus, now the congregation is mainly positioned to imitate Jesus himself in their ritual behavior toward one another. Their identities have taken a step toward soteriological fusion with the identity of Jesus.[18]

Placing the footwashing alongside the liturgy of the table and communion has the effect of shaping the way in which the meal *signifies*. Both in the Johannine and Lukan accounts, Jesus' mission is characterized as one of service and orientation toward the other. In eucharist, then, bread and wine are a participation in this priestly identity. The communion, Christ's body broken and blood poured out for the world, is taken into the bodies of those who are now, themselves, broken and poured out for the world. This is a function of the dance between the presence and absence of Christ in the eucharist. This ritual identification with the pattern of Jesus' life will be intensified in the Good Friday liturgy that follows.

The Maundy Thursday liturgy concludes, in most places, with the stripping of the altar and the removal of any remaining consecrated elements to a chapel or altar of repose. In addition to the evocation of solemnity by the divestment of the church's color, adornment, and illumination, the removal of the consecrated elements dramatically expresses the absence of Jesus who, in the narrative order of things, has been betrayed and removed from the people. The absence of Jesus is essential to the soteriological force of the people's worship, and I will give some attention to it below.[19] With the completion of the stripping of the altar, the people are now positioned to return, on the following day, to the passion gospel they heard on Palm Sunday—this time, however, with a markedly different relationship to Jesus' identity.

The Soteriological Fusion of Identities:
The Good Friday Liturgy

After the entry in silence, a collect revisits the "third person" relationship between the identity of the congregation and that of Jesus: the collect is prayed for the congregation as the family of God "for whom our Lord Jesus Christ was willing to be betrayed."[20] This recapitulates the theme of the people as responders and recipients of the work of Christ that dominated the Palm Sunday liturgy. They also listen again to the account of Jesus' crucifixion, as they did on Palm Sunday. Now, however, the reiteration of this third person relationship is situated between the Maundy

Thursday liturgy, in which the people define themselves by imitation of Jesus' identity, and the Solemn Collects of Good Friday, in which the people will take on that identity as the embodiment of Jesus' mission on behalf of the world. A much closer relationship between Christ and the assembly is now ritualized.

That intensified identification with Jesus is set up by the readings for the day. Three alternatives are provided for the Old Testament reading, all of which are rich with sacrificial imagery: the passages cover, respectively, the suffering servant of Isaiah, the sacrifice of Isaac, and the victimization of the righteous person.[21] The second lesson, taken from Hebrews 10, plays upon and focuses the sacrificial imagery on the person of Jesus Christ. He is both the sacrificial victim ("And it is by God's will that we have been sanctified through the offering of the body of Jesus Christ once for all") and the definitive high priest of the offering ("Therefore, my friends, since we have confidence to enter the sanctuary by the blood of Jesus...and since we have a great priest over the house of God, let us approach with a true heart in full assurance of faith....").[22] Following the epistle, the congregation hears the Johannine account of Jesus' passion and death. The connection of the priestly/sacrificial imagery of the preceding lessons and the reading of the Johannine account is not accidental: it is John's gospel that presents Jesus' ministry as a priestly act, and John's gospel in which Jesus prays his "high priestly prayer" before his arrest. This entire cluster of images contextualizes the assumption of Jesus' priestly identity by the people through the ritual acts that follow.

The Solemn Collects that immediately follow the homily are one of the two distinctive features of the Good Friday liturgy, and their structure plays a critical role in the soteriological fusion of identities between the people and Jesus as high priest. The Solemn Collects are the first specially crafted set of intercessions that the people have prayed since the liturgy for Ash Wednesday. The contrast between the two sets of prayers is extremely illuminating.

On Ash Wednesday, which initiates the preparatory period leading to Holy Week, the object of the Litany of Penitence is self-referential: the prayers focus largely on the faults of the people as they look to God for forgiveness. At first blush, one might expect the same sort of self-referential litany to be prescribed for Good Friday, since it focuses on the event through which, for Christians, forgiveness flows. In marked contrast to the Litany of Penitence, however, the Solemn Collects are directed outwardly to the world. The deacon (or other appointed intercessor) begins:

> Dear People of God: Our heavenly Father sent his Son into the world, not to condemn the world, but that the world through him might be saved; that all who believe in him might be delivered from the power of sin and death, and become heirs with him of everlasting life. We pray, therefore, for people everywhere according to their needs....[23]

This bidding is a critical hinge point in this liturgy. The overall structure of the bidding can be graphically presented this way:

The mission of Christ ⟶   Ecclesial mission

"We pray, therefore" is performative language by which the people, in prayer, are positioned to stand in the place of Jesus: their mission is the world's redemption. In the Solemn Collects, the people pray lengthy prayers for the church's witness and the world's needs with no reference to their own personal needs, save a closing petition for "the grace of a holy life." The ritual effect, congruent with the rite of the previous evening and intensifying the connection thus established between the identity of the people and that of Jesus, is to position the congregation as the embodiment and extension of Jesus' own high priestly ministry on behalf of the world, echoing the Johannine high priestly prayer on the eve of his death. Through this ritual identification, the church becomes Christ for the world, interceding on its behalf in love and compassion toward its travail.

Following the Solemn Collects, a wooden cross is brought into the church in full sight of the people, and placed in a visible location within the chancel or sanctuary. Local custom varies at this point, but the congregation, at the least, sings anthems in praise of the cross and in many places, in a continuation of early church practice, comes forward, one person at a time, to kiss the cross, kneel before it in prayer, or gaze upon it. At this point in the service, a congregation that has, over the course of two days, taken on Jesus' own high priestly ministry in the world now faces the ultimate symbol of that servant ministry: the mystery of God's presence to the world at the very place we most fear, the place of loss, suffering, and death. At the same time, loss, suffering, and death are not aggrandized or romanticized by this ritual because the adoration of the cross is situated within the larger movement of identity fusion toward which these liturgies have moved. The cross is not revered as the instrument of the world's redemption because of some inherent value in suffering itself: it is revered because death on the cross is the extent to which Jesus would go to live out his life of self-offering to the world. The cross is the ultimate act and symbol of that life of self-offering and, in revering the cross, the people revere the pattern of life of the Crucified.[24]

The Good Friday liturgy can continue, at this point, with communion from the sacrament reserved from the night before. In this context, the communion, juxtaposed with the Solemn Collects and Veneration of the Cross, reiterates the effect of the Maundy Thursday communion: the people receive the broken and saving body of Christ as they themselves are saved by willfully being broken and poured out for the world. The service concludes with a prayer that resituates the people, once again, in a third person relation with Christ, and makes the first and only explicit reference to the people's own need for forgiveness:

> Lord Jesus Christ, Son of the living God, we pray you to set your passion, cross, and death between your judgment and our souls, now and in the hour of our death. Give mercy and grace to the living; pardon and rest to the dead; to your holy Church peace and concord; and to us sinners everlasting life and glory; for with the Father and the Holy Spirit you live and reign, one God, now and forever. *Amen.*[25]

The End is in the Beginning: The Great Vigil of Easter

The Lighting of the Fire, Exsultet, and Vigil Readings

The Great Vigil is actually a construction of four different rites: the Lighting of the New Fire and Exsultet; the Vigil Readings; Holy Baptism; and the Holy Eucharist. As Gordon Lathrop argues, the juxtaposition of these four rituals and their constituent elements produces the meaning of the liturgy. Equally important is the lateral juxtaposition[26] of the Great Vigil as a whole to the Maundy Thursday and Good Friday liturgies.

The Great Vigil begins in the darkness of Easter eve, sometime between sunset on Saturday and sunrise on Easter morning. The celebrant initiates the liturgy with this address to the people, in which the gathering is caught up in the mystery of the passing over into freedom of the people of Israel and the passing over of Jesus from death to life:

> Dear friends in Christ: On this most holy night, in which our Lord Jesus passed over from death to life, the Church invites her members, dispersed throughout the world, to gather in vigil and prayer. For this is the Passover of the Lord, in which, by hearing

his Word and celebrating his Sacraments, we share in his victory
over death.[27]

This exhortation picks up and reiterates the priestly/sacrificial themes
of the Good Friday liturgy and Maundy Thursday's connection between
Jesus' passion and the passover, by which imagery the eucharistic meal
comes to be understood.[28] The celebrant then blesses the new fire, which
is carried into the darkened church by the deacon who chants three
times, at intervals, "The light of Christ." Then the Paschal Candle is
placed in its stand and the Exsultet is sung.[29]

The deacon begins the Exsultet by calling for the whole of creation—the heavens, the earth, and the church—to rejoice in "the victory of our mighty King."[30] Then, after a greeting between people and
deacon reminiscent of the *Sursum Corda* that begins the eucharistic
prayer,[31] the deacon continues in chant, recounting the deeds of God
in Christ: "This is the night, when you brought our fathers, the children of Israel, out of bondage in Egypt, and led them through the
Red Sea on dry land...." This curious grammatical structure has the
effect of inscribing the people within the narrative of salvation as a
story both past and continuing. Neither simple nostalgia nor mimesis, this portion of the liturgy enacts a faith that God is liberating at
this moment as we wait and watch for the second advent, yet does so
in the Christ who came. Watchfulness is a strong theme of the
Exsultet, alongside its celebration of the victory of Christ: the deacon
chants, "This is the night, when all who believe in Christ are delivered from the gloom of sin," yet also prays that Christ, "the Morning
Star who knows no setting, find [the candle] ever burning" at his second advent.

The watchful posture of the congregation is reinforced as they move
into the Liturgy of the Word, which begins with the words of the
Celebrant: "Let us hear the record of God's saving deeds in history, how

he saved His people in ages past; and let us pray that our God *will bring each of us to the fullness of redemption.*"[32]

Thankfulness for the work of salvation accomplished and the anticipation of the work yet to be done: these two themes sound in counterpoint throughout the Liturgy of the Word. This portion of the service, likely drawn from the synagogue pattern of readings and prayers, confers the quality of "vigil" on the Great Vigil of Easter.[33] The readings recount several of the key turning points in the story of God's saving relation to God's people: creation, the flood, the sacrifice of Isaac, the deliverance at the Red Sea, and the prophetic promises of Isaiah, Ezekiel, and Zephaniah.[34] Each is followed by an anthem or canticle, and concludes with a collect that makes clear that the paschal event is simultaneously a work accomplished and a work yet to be accomplished. For example, the reading of the creation story is accompanied by a response from psalmody that hymns the greatness of God's creation, and by this collect:

O God, who wonderfully created, and yet more wonderfully restored, the dignity of human nature: Grant that we may share in the divine life of him who humbled himself to share our humanity, your Son Jesus Christ our Lord.[35]

Baptism

From the vigil readings, the liturgy moves into Holy Baptism.[36] This rite is the primordial Christian initiatory rite, through which Christians are "buried with Christ in his death" and "share in his resurrection"[37] After the promises of the candidates to turn "from all the spiritual forces… which rebel against God," from "the evil powers of this world that corrupt and destroy the creatures of God," and from their own sins, the candidates promise to follow Christ as Lord and commit themselves to this faith by recitation of the Apostles' Creed.[38] Attached to the creed are promises that elaborate the commitments of the baptismal life: (1) continuation in the word and in eucharistic fellowship, (2) repentance and return to God whenever necessary, (3) proclamation of the gospel to the world, (4) service of Christ in all persons as an expression of the commandment to love the neighbor, and (5) work for justice, peace, and "the dignity of every human being." The last two of these significantly expand the forms of interrogation in earlier liturgies, calling for a breadth of ministry to every kind of need and awareness of the suffering of the human race. Baptism is not simply the erasure of the personal sin of the candidate, as it has in some cases been understood; rather, to serve all persons and to seek the dignity of every human being requires attentiveness to every manner and form of human suffering and need.

Immediately after these promises are made, the congregation offers prayers for the candidates. Depending upon the architecture of the space, the candidates may move bodily to the font as the prayers are offered, a powerful gestural symbol of the responsibility of the congregation for the new Christians who are about to be incorporated with them into the body of Christ. The structure of the prayers shares that soteriological logic of incorporation-into-mission we have seen in the *mandatum* and in the Solemn Collects of Good Friday:

(1) Deliver them, O Lord, from the way of sin and death…
(2) Open their hearts to your grace and truth…
(3) Fill them with your holy and life-giving Spirit…
(4) Keep them in the faith and communion of your holy Church…
(5) Teach them to love others in the power of the Spirit…
(6) Send them into the world in witness to your love…
(7) Bring them to the fullness of your peace and glory…[39]

The hinge point of the petitions is prayer 3, a clear reference to the gift of the Spirit given in baptism, by which they enter into communion with others who share baptismal identity, referred to in petition 4. Petitions 1 and 2 are preparatory and petitions 5 and 6 flesh out the nature of the mission to which they are called in baptism; 7 announces the hope toward which this life leads. The prayers are concluded with a collect in which the theme of incorporation of Christ predominates: "Grant, O Lord, that all who are baptized into the death of Jesus Christ your Son may live in the power of his resurrection and look for him to come again in glory; who lives and reigns, now and forever. *Amen.*"[40]

The Thanksgiving over the Water links the water of baptism with the waters of creation, with those through which the people of Israel passed in their liberation from bondage, and to Christ's own baptism in which he was "anointed by the Holy Spirit" as Christ. Those baptized are "buried with Christ in his death" and "share in his resurrection." The celebrant then touches the water and prays: "Now sanctify this water…by the power of your Holy Spirit, that those who here are cleansed from sin and born again may continue for ever in the risen life of Jesus Christ our Savior…."[41]

The post-baptismal portion of the rite includes an anointing accompanied by an affirmation of the candidate's being "sealed by the Holy Spirit" and a welcome by the congregation to confess and proclaim the resurrection and share in Christ's priesthood. The association of the anointing with the Spirit, by whom Christ was also anointed in baptism by the Spirit, with whom the candidates will be "filled" at baptism (according to the prayers outlined above) creates a soteriological red thread of incorporation into Christ's identity and participation in his priestly mission. The baptism occurs at this point in the Triduum and not a moment earlier: in the Maundy Thursday and Good Friday liturgies, the people have rehearsed bodily the truth that life is found in self-offering, and have taken on the identity of the suffering servant on behalf of the world. Only now are the contours of the life to which they are called completely clear. Baptism is not a mental assent to certain truths. It is, at one and the same time, the culmination of bodily practices in which a certain identity is assumed, and the initiation of continuing growth into that identity. The "share" in Christ's resurrection into which Christians are initiated is anything but the closure or overcoming of struggle and suffering, but its transfiguration.

Liturgy of the Word and the Eucharist

After the baptism, presider and people proclaim: "Alleluia. Christ is risen. The Lord is risen indeed. Alleluia." Following hymns of praise and a Collect for Easter, the people resume the story of God's saving work through Christ, moving from the Old Testament to a reading from the Epistle to the Romans. In this Epistle, which is not optional, the people hear again what they have practiced with their bodies. It underlines the unfinished nature of the way of suffering and the promise that life comes in and through that way:

> Do you not know that all of us who have been baptized into Christ Jesus were baptized into his death? Therefore we have been buried with him by baptism into death, so that, just as Christ was raised from the dead by the glory of the Father, so we too might walk in newness of life....But if we have died with Christ, we believe that we will also live with him.[42]

The people then hear the gospel of Matthew, which tells of the encounter between an angel and the women at the empty tomb and the promise of the risen Christ's appearance to the disciples in Galilee. A people only too aware that they are still subject to suffering and physical death can hear the post-resurrection account as a note of hope that their suffering and death have been transformed as the doorway to life by the wounded yet risen Christ. That our passing over into life with Christ comes not after, beyond, or even in spite of suffering and struggle, but through it, is a mystery that continues to deepen as we watch and wait for the second advent. The church's participation in the paschal mystery becomes a continual openness to God's presence in our suffering, and of God's presence to others in *their* suffering through *our* presence to them. Here, the ritual positioning of the congregation in the two preceding liturgies comes to its full fruition in the Easter liturgy.

Following the homily, the congregation moves into the first Eucharist of Easter. This eucharist brings the liturgical action of the Triduum full circle: the Paschal Triduum began with a eucharist in which the people came to grips with the way of life as the way of suffering; it ends with a eucharist celebrating that the way of suffering, mysteriously, gives way to life. The eucharistic prayer is a thanksgiving for redemption and a prayer for the empowerment of the congregation to take their mission into the world. Yet always at the heart of the prayer are Jesus' words over the bread and wine, which are associated with his suffering and death. In their communion, the people take this very life into their own bodies as they, paradoxically, are thereby incorporated into his body.[43] Here, again, church assumes the identity of Christ's own body in the world—the same identity of servant to the suffering world as that practiced in the *mandatum* of Thursday—in the Solemn Collects of Good Friday—into which they were incorporated by baptism. Far from overcoming or eliminating the problem of suffering, each one of these liturgies begins and ends in the liminal reality of human suffering, finding the power of life in and through it and finding the strength to face it.

The importance of the eucharistic dimension of the Maundy Thursday and Easter Vigil liturgies requires closer attention to two matters: eucharistic presence and the eucharistic prayer. First, however, let us linger over Holy Saturday.

Holy Saturday

Although the Triduum as a liturgical experience focuses around the three
major liturgies we have outlined, the Triduum as temporal duration (the
"three days") includes Holy Saturday as well, for which a very spare
proper liturgy is provided in the Anglican tradition. The liturgy of the
American prayer book provides readings that enunciate the themes of
ascetical preparation for Easter, the acknowledgment of mortality, and
the burial of Christ. It provides for an optional anthem thought to date
from the tenth century ("In the midst of life we are in death…"), an
anthem also used in the burial office. The service is brief, almost conveying a sense of bafflement at what one should do with oneself in this liminal moment. Yet this liminality is close to the heart of the "indivisible
mystery" of suffering and salvation and, at the same time (and for that
reason), nearly impermeable to theological explication. We live, stretched
between suffering and salvation, living in the latter through hope, even in
the midst of the former, and its pain—the very condition of humanity
that we are in the process of identifying as the form of life sanctified by
the Triduum liturgies as the arena of God's work. George Steiner speaks
to this sabbatarian existence of ours:

> There is one particular day in Western history about which neither
> historical record nor myth nor Scripture make report. It is a
> Saturday. And it has become the longest of days. We know of that
> Good Friday which Christianity holds to have been that of the
> Cross….We know also about Sunday…. But ours is the long day's
> journey of the Saturday…. The apprehensions and figurations in
> the play of metaphysical imagining, in the power and the music,
> which tell of pain and of hope, of the flesh which is said to taste of
> ash and of the spirit which is said to have the savour of fire, are
> always Sabbatarian. They have risen out of an immensity of wait-

ing, which is that of man. Without them, how could we be patient?[44]

Steiner's eloquent testimony to the power and meaning of art applies as well to the Triduum liturgies. For in those liturgies is the power to form and shape a life that is patient in suffering—acknowledging its horror yet not fearing to face its reality—not, as Steiner elsewhere implies, because this sabbatarian existence is a "long day's journey" that leads finally to the triumph of good, but because it is the very habitation of humanity in which good has been wrought by God. Into this very sabbatarian existence, God has come to be present in solidarity with us, with life outpoured in the suffering service of the Son, whose suffering service is *life*. Holy Saturday is the day in which God has died "into" our very own death and sanctified it, in all its stark, immovable threat. Holy Saturday is the truth of our lives, so close to where we are that it serves as the heart of the paschal liturgies but is itself, as the very nature of the divine-human encounter, a mystery beyond even the power of liturgy to encode.

Could this be why Holy Saturday has been observed with rather spare liturgical elaboration in the churches of the west?[45] On the classical premise that any event in the life of Christ is, at some level, a trinitarian event—that God is at work, involved in and impacted by whatever is experienced or done by Christ[46]—then the death of the Son is the very entry of God into human suffering and death. Here, we stand at the very edge of human understanding. Holy Saturday marks the deep and astounding mystery that is the pasch: the place in-between, where the eternal God, the divine source of all life, joins and "dissolves" in loss, death, and catastrophe. The Christian tradition has sometimes associated the in-between time of Holy Saturday with Christ's descent into hell. Situated between the liturgies that precede and follow it, however, this descent is not sequentially but rather existentially related to God's work of salvation in Christ. That is, one could see God's descent in Christ as an unpleasant but necessary step toward securing the resurrected life for humanity; but, consistent with the more subtle and dynamic interaction of life and death we are beginning to see in the structure of the Triduum liturgies, one understands Holy Saturday as a symbol of the power of life breaking forth "inside" of death, as it were, because God participates even in death. God saves us in our suffering and dying because God himself *is* in our suffering.

In the course of interpreting Gregory the Great and Isidore of Seville, Hans Urs von Balthasar comments: "he [Christ] is, objectively speaking, whilst in the midst of the darkness of what is contrary to God, in 'paradise'...."[47] In another place, von Balthasar speaks poetically in an imagined conversation between Christ and the human person. Christ speaks:

You leap down from a high cliff. The leap is freely made, and yet, the moment you leap, gravity leaps upon *you*, and you tumble exactly like a dead stone to the bottom of the gorge. This is how I decided to give myself. To give myself right out of my hand....The Consumed, the Eaten, the Drunk, the Spilled, the Poured Out. The Plaything. The Worn Out. The one squeezed to the very dregs. The one trod upon to infinity. The one run over. The one thinned to air. The one liquified into an ocean. The Dissolved. This was the plan; this was the will of the Father. By fullfilling it through obedience (the fulfillment itself was obedience), I have filled the world from heaven down to hell....Now I am all in all, and this is why the death which poured me out is victory. My descent, my vertiginous collapse, my going under (under myself) into everything that was foreign and contrary to God—down into the underworld: this was the ascent of this world into me, into God....You are in God—at the price of my own Godhead. You have love—I lost it to you....This was my victory. In the Cross was Easter.[48]

To understand this is to understand only as a glimmer: here is the very abyss into which even the rich valences of liturgical enactment and code cannot venture. It is for this reason that we step lightly over Holy Saturday in this study—indeed, the reason why the western tradition of this day has been spare, or non-existent: at one level, it is the heart of the Paschal Mystery that we will put into words; at another, it is the very heart of the divine life in life-emptied, a mystery at which the human intellect, even as exercised through ritual practice, stands dumbfounded and in awe. In the end, the silence of Holy Saturday points to this mystery.

The Presence of Christ in the Eucharistic Sacrament

The eucharist involves a sacramental consumption of blessed bread and wine that signifies, for the church, the ethical shape of the church's life as a paschal people, itself broken and poured out for the life of the world. This consumption occurs as a high point in the larger context of Maundy Thursday and the Easter Vigil in which the work of Christ is enacted by the liturgical assembly in full-bodied participation. This meaning of the eucharistic action is articulated memorably by Augustine:

> So if you want to understand the body of Christ, listen to the apostle telling the faithful, *You, though, are the body of Christ and its members* (1 Cor 12:27). So if it's you that are the body of Christ and its members, it's the mystery meaning you that has been placed on the Lord's table....It is to what you are that you reply *Amen*, and by so replying you express your assent. What you hear, you see, *is The body of Christ*, and you answer *Amen*. So be a member of the body of Christ, in order to make that *Amen* true....Be what you can see, and receive what you are.[49]

Interpreting Augustine, William T. Cavanaugh comments:

> …the eucharist is much more than a ritual repetition of the past. It
> is rather a literal re-membering of Christ's body, a knitting together
> of the Body of Christ by the participation of many in his sacri-
> fice….Christ adopted the form of a servant. His self-gift to human-
> ity, his complete *kenosis*, is such that he gives over his very identity
> to the community of his followers, who thereby become in history
> His true body, which in turn takes the form of a servant. The
> Christian sacrifice unites us both to each other and to God in the
> Body of Christ, so that we become what is offered on the altar. This,
> says Augustine, is the import of the Eucharist.[50]

Theologies of transubstantiation, transignification, memorial, and the
like are all ways in which one attempts to understand how Christ is present in mysterious form in the eucharist. Their risk, if not expressed with
care, is in making the eucharist a fetish, a pure presence that inspires
inaction and adoration of the eucharist itself, rather than ethical action
and formation into a paschal people as the church is called.

To put this another way, the identity of the people, who come to
assume the identity and mission of Christ in the Triduum liturgies, is
founded both on the presence and the absence of Christ. The presence of
Christ in the eucharist for the church is not a pure or simple presence,
but a complex presence that appears under the mode of absence.
Proclaimed in the liturgies of the word and in their intercessory response
to what is proclaimed, received in the sacramental signs of water, oil,
bread, and wine, and enacted in the congregation's servant life directed
toward their neighbors both inside and outside the church, Christ's presence is not fully exhausted by any one of these manifestations, including
the consecrated bread and wine of the eucharist. In each of these liturgical forms, Christ is both present and absent—present, as one shaping

ecclesial ethics and as the one to whom the church responds; absent as one who removes himself from priestly service to the world so that the church can become that priestly presence. It is this dynamic interaction of presence and absence that *produces the church* that Louis-Marie Chauvet addresses:

> To give up hope of finding the lost body of Jesus by consenting to meet him, alive, in the symbolic mediation of the Church thus requires a good joining of the three elements [of Christ in the Scriptures, Christ in the sacraments, and Christ in our brothers and sisters] in their mutual differences. Without this, one would become fixated on one or the other and enclose oneself imaginatively in it, insisting that Christ must reside there. Now, as risen, Christ has departed; we must agree to this loss if we want to be able to find him. To agree to this loss, as we said, is equivalent to consenting to its symbol: the Church.[51]

In addition to founding the church's identity as Christ to the world, this absence also founds its resistance to the ideological fetish that it is the one and privileged place of Christ—a fetish that inevitably leads to the church abandoning its paschal identity of solidarity with those who suffer and, instead, producing suffering by arrogating to itself a divine authority that it does not have. In other words, the absence of Christ in the eucharist has both critical and formative effect. It is formative in that the church receives its identity from Christ who has withdrawn from them in order to grant it; it is critical in that it resists the church's imperialist confusion of itself with Christ. Again, Chauvet:

> This is why to consent to the sacramental mediation of the Church is to consent to what we called above, echoing Heidegger, *the presence of the absence of God.* The Church radicalizes the vacancy of the

place of God. To accept its mediation is to agree that this vacancy
will never be filled....But it is precisely in the act of respecting his
radical absence or otherness that the Risen One can be recogized
symbolically. For this is the faith; this is Christian identity according to the faith.[52]

The presence of Christ in the eucharist as a presence-in-absence is recognized by other interpreters beside Chauvet: Robert Sokolowski provides a phenomenology of disclosure that shows how presence and
absence, far from being opposed, are related in complex fashion, so that
God transcends any single presentation that produces a new kind of
absence (an absence in faith), an expectation of a new kind of presence
(in hope), and a new possibility of identification (in charity).[53] David
Power shows how the re-presentation of Christ in the eucharist involves,
like any other symbolic mediation, "distance within the being present."[54]
And Catherine Pickstock argues that the very distinction between presence and absence is a result of the immanentist interpretation of signs
characteristic of postmodernist philosophers—a flattening of the sign
that Pickstock claims is "outwitted" by eucharistic presence.[55] In each
case, the eucharist is recognized as conveying complex, not pure or
simple, presence of Christ, and this complexity is very much operative in
the eucharistic celebrations within the Triduum. Each in their own way
is arguing for the simultaneously critical and formative power of the
eucharistic action.

Augustine sees in Scripture a testimony to a kind of three-fold presence of Christ in his eternal nature as God, in the God-Man Jesus, and
in the church. Prior to the taking of flesh, Christ is the eternal Word of
God, present to all and everywhere yet undivided, analogous to the way
in which a concept can be held in the mind of persons separated by distance, yet understood in its totality by each.[56] A non-identical, yet non-
contradictory claim is made of Christ that he is present in the mediator,

in whom he "began to be man but, indeed, did not cease to be God."[57] In this mode, both humanity and divinity are present to one another; more precisely, humanity is caught up in the divine life, "so that [human beings] might see what he never lost as a result of what he took on."[58] In a third manner of presence, without detracting from each of these claims, he is taken to be the mystical head of the church:

> Not that he isn't complete without the body, but that he was pre-pared to be complete and entire together with us too, though even without us he is always complete and entire, not only insofar as he is the Word…but also in the very man whom he took on, and with whom he is both God and man together. All the same, brothers and sisters, how are we his body, and he one Christ with us?….All of us together are the members of Christ and his body; not only those of us who are in this place, but throughout the whole world….From Abel the just, right up to the end of the world, as long as people beget and are begotten, any of the just who make this passage through life, all that now—that is, not in this place, but in this life—all that are going to be born after us, all constitute the one body of Christ….[59]

What is significant for our purposes here is Augustine's care not to reduce these modes of Christ's presence to one, but to proclaim these as three irreducible modes of Christ's presence that emerge from narrative shape of the Scripture[60]—his presence to the Father, to humanity, and in the church.[61]

> Thus it is then that sometimes in the Scriptures Christ is presented in such a way that you are to understand him as the Word equal to the Father; in such a way sometimes that you are to understand him as the mediator, since *the Word became flesh to dwell amongst us* (Jn

1:14)....Sometimes, though, in such a way that you are to understand the head and the body....[62]

This has the effect of confounding the tendency to claim any one as
the place where Christ is uniquely to be found. He is both fully present,
yet not exhaustively present, in any one. Each way of speaking about
Christ's presence has, as it were, a shadow of absence about it, arising
from the refusal of Scripture to valorize one way of speaking of Christ
over others. To the extent that the sacrament of eucharist is the *signum*
of the materiality of the God-man, who is its *res*, it must at the same time
be complemented by the practice of Christ's own life by the church as its
res as well. The permanent tension generated by the three-fold manner
of Scriptural speech about Christ makes it possible that, in the sacrament
of his body given for the life of the world, "the faithful know the body of
Christ if they should not neglect to be the body of Christ."[63]

Graham Ward provides a more contemporary theological account of
Christ's eternal, material/sacramental, and mystical body, suggesting that
the gospel narratives *systematically* displace and resituate the meaning of
the body of Jesus, and make his presence complex and manifold. Ward's
particular concern is with the way in which the gender of Jesus' body is
increasingly impossible to appropriate in simplicity, but his point maintains the theological notion exemplified by Augustine and others that
Jesus Christ cannot be appropriated under one mode of presence, and that
this very fact is generative of the church's identity as "Christ" in the world.

According to Ward, as the narrative of the gospels unfold, we begin
with the curious bodily character of the God-Man born from a virgin,
gendered and subject to normal human limitations of infirmity and locality, yet also existing in the stretch between Adam's corporeality and the
resurrected body that he will ultimately assume.[64] As the narrative
unfolds, Jesus is transfigured, breaking the boundaries of a merely male-
gendered beauty by a manifestation of divine beauty beyond the body.[65]

On the night before he dies, he offers his body as bread and bread as his body in the institution of the eucharist, which marks the turn from these transformations of his physical body to the transformation of his disciples' bodies as he offers his own body to theirs: "…it is not that Jesus, at this point, stops being a physical presence. It is more that his physical presence can extend itself to incorporate other bodies, like bread, and make them extensions of their own."[66] This he does by his self-surrender, which he extends to the crucifixion through which his own body is the body of all those who have suffered and longed for God, and for whom we mourn. At the same time, by Christ's crucifixion, our illusory attachment to those other bodies is broken and we come to know in him the illusion of our self-unity and the givenness of all bodies, including our own, to others:

> It is not simply that the physical body of Jesus is displaced in the Christian story; our bodies, too, participate in that displacement in and through the crucifixion. At the eucharist we receive and we are acted upon: now, having brought into relation and facing the acknowledgement of the breaking of that relation we recognize displacement of the body as part of Christian living….The eucharistic fracture, repeating differently the crucifixion, disseminates the body—of Christ and the Church as the body of Christ. The dissemination sets each body free to follow (and both be transposed and transfigured) within the plenitude of the Word which passes by and passes on. What initiates the following after is our awareness of being involved, of our having been drawn into the ongoing divine activity. Our being involved is a tasting of that which we know we long for; we drink of eternal life in that participation.[67]

So, our participation through eucharist in the crucifixion, which displaces and disseminates the presence of Christ to the disciples and the world to whom he surrenders himself in love, gathers us into the same dissemination for the world's sake: ecclesial identity poured out for the world as the very point at which that identity is established. Participating in that divine activity, that outpouring of our lives for other lives, is the nature of being church and *is* eternal life.

This entire Christian narrative is told, of course, from the point of view of the resurrection, which is the icon and actuality of Christ's displaced and disseminated presence as positive, as eternal Life. This includes the empty tomb, at which his presence is announced in the gospel of John by the framing of his absence with angels at either end of the place where his body lay—the resurrection appearances in which he both is and is not locally present and recognizable—and the gospel narrative itself, which is not simply a category of the narrative genre but faithfully renders the displaced presences of Jesus by following him to, and announcing, his very disappearance in the ascension.[68]

The "logic of the ascension," in fact, marks the whole of the gospel and gives birth to the church, understood as the "Logos creating a space within himself, a womb, within which (*en Christoi*) the Church will expand and creation be recreated....In this way, the body of the Church and the body of the world are enfolded through resurrection within the Godhead....The body of Jesus Christ is not lost, nor does it reside now in heaven as a discrete object for veneration...." To locate Jesus there or, for that matter, on the plane of historical reconstruction or stable metaphysical foundation is pointless because "the Church is now the body of Christ, so to understand the body of Jesus we can only examine what the Church is and what it has to say concerning the nature of that body as Scripture attests to it. The Church dwells in Christ and in Christ works out its salvation and the salvation of the world."[69]

Whether approaching Christ's presence in the eucharist from a phenomenological standpoint, from the classic theological position of Augustine on the triple mode of Christ's presence, or from Ward's soteriological reflection on Jesus' disseminated body, one sees that the saving relation enacted in the Triduum between Christ and the church is the one formed as much by absence as by simple presence. All are rooted, too, in the deep preoccupation of scripture that reflects, as Robert Brawley describes, "the struggle of early Christians to come to grips with the mystery of how believers stand in a relationship with the risen Christ who is now absent."[70] In all these cases, the paschal identity of the church as "Christ for the world" presumes a felicitous, manifold quality of the presence and absence of Christ that stretches the normal boundaries of the time past and present (as in anamnetic remembrance) and of space and place. The deep grammar of the Triduum is a "logic of the Ascension": Christ is withdrawn from the world so that the church can be the church, mediating the presence of Christ to the world by itself embodying his servant Life. At the same time, this form of life constitutes salvation precisely because, as the Triduum celebrates, all our suffering and longing is caught up in Christ and transfigured as the way to Life in God.[71]

The Structure of the Eucharistic Prayer

Not only the phenomenological relationship between presence and absence but the structure of the eucharistic prayers contribute to the soteriology of the Triduum liturgies. Of the seven eucharistic anaphoras appropriate for use at Maundy Thursday and the Great Vigil of Easter,[72] six manifest the West Syrian anaphoral structure. The predominance of the West Syrian structure in eucharistic prayers of the Episcopal Church has been a long time in coming. Picked up from the Scottish tradition that influenced the American prayer books,[73] this structure in its mature form generally contains the following elements and order:

Sursum corda
Preface, Sanctus, Benedictus

Post-Sanctus with Institution Narrative
Anamnesis/oblation
Supplication with Epiclesis and Intercessions
Final Doxology and People's Amen

The historical and geographical variants of this prayer are a fascinating study in themselves.[74] For our purposes, what is significant is the theology of the West Syrian anaphoral structure and its resonance with the paschal soteriology of the Triduum.

The account of salvation history, typically appearing in the preface and much more in the post-Sanctus, is quite strong in the West Syrian prayer. Beginning with the praise of God as creator and Lord over the myriad orders of the universe, God is hymned in the Sanctus and Benedictus, which links the acclamation of God's holiness in Isaiah 6 with the Lukan acclamation of Jesus upon his entry into Jerusalem. This linkage between the transcendent, holy God with the man Jesus, who enters the holy city to suffer and die, is not unique to the West Syrian prayer, but may have first appeared there. It is a key to an incarnational theology in which the mission of Jesus instantiates the covenant between people and God and reflects the Jewish and Christian understanding of earthly worship as a part of the heavenly liturgy.

The strong account of salvation history comes next in the prayer. The post-Sanctus in which it appears is the context for the account of the institution narrative. All this history of God's saving acts toward us function, in turn, as the warrant for our prayer around this table, now. The link between our prayer and the earlier recitation of thanksgiving is the anamnesis and oblation, an element variously worded whose logic is this: "remembering, we offer." This focuses the entire prayer as our responsive act of God: the gifts of ourselves and of bread and wine are return gifts, offered in celebration of the holiness of God and God's saving acts toward us, supremely manifested in Christ. While the term *anamnesis* refers here to this specific rhetorical link between the thanksgiving and the supplication to which the prayer now turns, the entire prayer is anamnetic. The term refers to remembrance that is neither longing for a lost past (nostalgia) nor repetition of the past to secure anxiety and restore order in the present (mimesis), but prayer for our work in the present as anticipation of the eschatological future. The key to that future is in *the memory of what God has done*. Indeed, this is Metz's "future in the memory of suffering." The liturgical assembly calls for the power of the Spirit to make of them the signs of that future as they are strengthened by Christ in the sacrament.[75] The intercessory dimension of that work, like that which occurs in the Solemn Collects, is to begin immediately, before the anaphora has even concluded.

The eucharistic prayers of the 1979 prayer book, with the exception of one, all mainly manifest this West Syrian pattern. The older prayers of the traditional eucharistic rite, largely reflecting the language of Thomas Cranmer's reformation prayers, focus rather narrowly on sin as the "problem" toward which Jesus' saving work is directed. The more commonly used prayers of the newer rite (from which the eucharistic prayer of the Triduum would be drawn) hardly ignore sin, but broaden the soteriological concen of Jesus' work to include poverty, sadness, error, bondage, and the power of death. This broader imagery of the human problem, even when linked to sin, is typical of eucharistic prayers prior to the early middle ages. Not all the eucharistic prayers of the 1979 prayer book include the intercessions of the West Syrian pattern, but in Prayer D—the most fulsome example of that pattern—the work for which the church asks the Spirit's empowerment begins even before the prayer has concluded.

What may we say, then, about the theology of the West Syrian anaphora as it shapes these eucharistic prayers and relates to the other elements of the Triduum? First, the anthropology of the prayer is one in which people *come to be who they are* by anamnetic remembrance. Second, that remembrance includes the recalling of suffering that lies, not simply before it, but at its very heart. Third, this remembrance includes the whole sweep of salvation through history and so calls to mind, both within and beyond the prayer, how God has reached out to sorrow, suffering, sin, catastrophe, and loss. Finally, anamnetic remembrance is a moral act. It is connected to a way of life, whose outlines have been sketched in the baptismal liturgy as an incorporation into Christ. These theological features of the West Syrian anaphora are thoroughly resonant with what we have seen in the rest of the Triduum.

Taking Stock

It is useful to pause briefly at this point to take stock of what we have seen so far. This brief review both summarizes the foregoing observations on the structure and soteriology of the Triduum and forms the background to further analysis in Chapter Five.

So far, we have attempted to illuminate the saving relation between Christ and the church as it emerges from within the structure of the Triduum liturgies and in their juxtaposition to one another. We have seen how the symbols, actions, and themes of each refer back and forth across the three days to the other two. We have seen how baptism acts as an entry into a form of life, an embodiment of the life of Christ as a priestly servant of the world's need and suffering. We have seen how both the structure of the eucharistic prayers and the dynamic relationship between presence and absence make a way for this very same embodiment.

Each of the liturgies has its own focus, yet in relation to each of the others. Maundy Thursday enacts the shape of Christian discipleship as one marked by the outpouring of servant love to the world. The footwashing draws the congregation into the symbolic action with which Jesus underlined the nature of this fellowship with him. The institution of the eucharist, in which his body and blood are "given for" us, connects the final sacrifice of his life with the broader self-sacrifice that marked his entire ministry and to which we are called as disciples.

This provides the context for the Good Friday liturgy: without the observance of Maundy Thursday, Good Friday would leave the passion and crucifixion like a "dangling modifer" to Jesus' life, a tragic end to which he came despite his best efforts to serve. Juxtaposed with the Maundy Thursday liturgy, Jesus' suffering and death are seen as both the ultimate act and symbol of his entire life and self-offering—the act in which Jesus "completes upon the cross the sacrifice of his life."[76] At the same time, the Good Friday liturgy presumes that this life of self-offering, in which Jesus does not shrink from the cross to which that life leads him, opens counter-intuitively into a new and transformed life that cannot be extinguished, even by the grave. The celebration of the resurrection is presumed by the Good Friday liturgy: thus the veneration of the cross which, in and of itself, is only an instrument of torture and death. This way of self-offering that does not shrink from suffering becomes the way of life, grounding the baptism of the catechumens at Easter, through which they are "buried with Christ…in his death…."[77] As we have seen, the baptismal action is completed by the eucharist which, like the eucharist of Maundy Thursday, is the sacramental extension of the self-giving presence of Jesus into which the whole church is called in his absence.

Some Concluding Observations on the Triduum

In the next chapter, we will consider paschal soteriology from other angles, exploring the liturgy as soteriology, revisiting and deepening our sense of the soteriology of the liturgy in relation to other disciplines, and suggesting the contribution of this paschal soteriology to the wider conversation in this theological discipline. Two final remarks remain to be made before we proceed to that task. First, I wish to point out the

inadequacy of one "classical" approach to ritual interpretation in relation to the Triduum liturgies. Secondly, I offer a comment on the fruit-
fulness and the limitations of the Lathropian approach to liturgy that I
have adapted for this analysis.

The Inadequacy of Abstract Models of Ritual Action

There is a commonly held opinion, arising from the work of a number of
influential anthropologists and social psychologists, that the function of
ritual can be succinctly stated in a manner such as this: participants enter
the ritual context with a certain identity, which is creatively disintegrated
by the ritual passage through a state of liminality from which the participant emerges with a new identity stasis in which the self-relation and
social relation of the participant is reconstituted in a new form. This
movement from stasis, through liminal space, to new and transformed
stasis, is often associated with initiation into a particular social community or the passage from one stage of psychosocial development to
another. While his interpretation of ritual becomes somewhat nuanced
over time, Victor Turner's work is associated with this approach to ritual
interpretation, as is the structuralist approach of Arnold van Gennep that
lies behind it.[78]

The problem with this classical framework is that it must, in order to
work, abstract from the specific content of any given ritual. If the meaning of a ritual is a function of its structure and *content*, then this classical
model misses ritual meaning by abstracting from the ritual specificity of
any particular tradition. Both the utility and the limitation of the classical model is this abstraction from specificity.

Consider the case of the Triduum liturgies. If one interprets the
Triduum along the lines of this structuralist theory, without giving specific attention to the elements within the rites and their internal configuration, the ritual appears to line up quite nicely with a three-step

movement from identity, through liminal passage, to new identity.[79] Jesus begins with an identity as teacher and healer (Maundy Thursday), passes through a liminal cauldron of betrayal, abandonment, and suffering (Good Friday), and emerges as the quintessential symbol of new identity: resurrected Lord, passing beyond suffering and death into eternal life (Easter). The purpose of this ritual for the congregation would be a reenactment of the same passage through liminality into a state of victory over suffering and death.

In fact, as I have tried to show, this is not at all what the Triduum liturgies do. The Triduum liturgies are anything but a movement from one identity, through liminality, to a new identity. The liturgies of Maundy Thursday and Good Friday are not preparatory steps for the ritual climax of Easter; rather, the Great Vigil of Easter, Maundy Thursday, and Good Friday refer back and forth across one another as different ritual enactments of the same mystery of life's emergence in and through suffering. Maundy Thursday celebrates the tender compassion of teacher and disciples toward one another around table fellowship, but does so in the shadow of impending catastrophe; Good Friday lingers at the foot of the cross because life is mysteriously found there, as Jesus taught on Thursday and as the resurrection symbolizes on Sunday; the Great Vigil of Easter proclaims the resurrected Christ in the midst of a world still suffering, struggling, and waiting for remedy. *In short, the Triduum liturgies begin, continue, and end in a liminal place.* In contrast to the interpretation that the classical model yields, the mutual inter-signification of these three liturgies offers a more complex, but finally more realistic consolation, because it forms people who are prepared to face reality we know all too well. There is no gospel for the people of Bosnia or Sierra Leone, or for those who suffer the darkness of depression, or for any of us, if we must wait for suffering to resolve into a state of grace beyond it, where divine fullness of life waits for us. Their salvation, and the salvation of Christians, is to face those who suffer and see the truth: God is *there*, and redemption occurs *there*, as we stand in the place of Christ with those who suffer.

The Lathropian Approach to Liturgical Theology

I began this chapter with a promise to analyze the liturgies of the Triduum by adapting Lathrop's analysis of juxtaposition. I have done so, looking not only at the juxtaposition of elements within each liturgy but, in congruence with the early church's instinct for their indissolubility, looking at the juxtaposition of the three liturgies as a unitary phenomenon. I have used Lathrop's own language, opening up the structural arrangement of these liturgies to reveal what they *mean* or *signify*. I am now in a position to say that this Lathropian language, while useful, needs to be qualified in a way with which, I believe, Lathrop would be sympathetic. The soteriological force of liturgy is not so much in what it *means*, but in what it *does*. In the Triduum liturgies, the people enter into saving relation with Christ by taking on his identity. This is so, not because they think about it, or consider what such an assumption of Jesus' identity might mean, but because the liturgy maneuvers them into that position, and maneuvers them bodily: the people stand, speak, kneel, wash, eat, listen, kiss or touch the cross, and process through the darkness. In the liturgy, the people become Christ to the world through the patterned action of their bodies. This suggests an anthropology in which, as Rebecca Chopp puts it in a *festschrift* for Don E. Saliers, we work "from the body through language to deeds."[80] In attending closely to the liturgy for the shape of a theological response to suffering, we are seeking first not a set of propositions that can be extracted, but for the constitutive bodily actions through which people are oriented to face suffering in a certain way. The meaning of the Triduum liturgies is finally in what they do to form a people in this way.

As we turn, in the next chapter, to further analysis of the Triduum's soteriology, we do well to remember that what the liturgy *means* is found in what it *does*. While a soteriology will necessarily be developed in a propositional form, it concerns itself, in the final analysis, not with a set of ideas but with the shape of a life.

Notes

1. Gordon Lathrop, *Holy Things: A Liturgical Theology* (Minneapolis: Fortress, 1993), 33.

2. Ibid., 36–44.

3. Ibid., 40.

4. He reconciles this methodology with his Lutheran commitment to the Word by claiming that the pattern of liturgical juxtaposition is consistent with the textual juxtaposition of the Bible.

5. Ibid., 32.

6. I will reserve comment on the Ash Wednesday liturgy until we address the prayers of Good Friday, to which Ash Wednesday's litany is of particular relevance.

7. Examples of these liturgies can be found in the Episcopal *Book of Occasional Services*, 55ff. Their observance varies widely with local custom and they will not detain us here.

8. An account of the gradual linkage of the palm procession with the passion account is provided by Stevenson, *Jerusalem Revisited*, 18ff.

9. *Book of Common Prayer* (*BCP*), 271.

10. Ibid., 272.

11. Ibid.

12. Ibid., 274.

13. 1 Corinthians 11:23–26

14. Rubrics allow for reading Luke's institution narrative, which we will consider below. However, the Corinthian account of the eucharist and the Johannine foot-washing account are traditional for the evening eucharist on this day, as reflected in the earliest Roman lectionaries.

15. The posture of imitation is suggested by the name of the day, which has been a custom since at least the seventh century: "Maundy" is derived from *mandatum* or commandment. The reference is to the "new commandment" of Jesus in John 13:34: "I give you a new commandment, that you love one another. *Just as I have loved you, you also should love one another*" (emphasis added). See Hatchett, *Commentary on the American Prayer Book*, 229.

16. John 13:12–15.

17. *Book of Occasional Services* (New York: The Church Hymnal Corporation, 1994), 93.

18. Although the ritual action of the people is less dramatic, the same dynamic occurs in this liturgy even when local custom focuses more on the supper than on the footwashing. The alternative gospel, the Lukan account of the institution, concludes with the disciples argument over "which one of them was to be regarded as the greatest" and Jesus' exhortation to serve one another as he has done.

19. See the selection on eucharistic presence, pp. 71–79.

20. *BCP*, 276.

21. Isaiah 52:13–53:12; Genesis 22:1–18; Wisdom 2:1, 12–24.

22. From Hebrews 10:1–25. This has been the designated Epistle reading since the first Anglican prayer book of 1549. See Hatchett, *Commentary*, 234. The soteriology of the Triduum contributes something to wider discussions in soteriology through its concerns about the sacrificial imagery of Jesus' death. We will consider this in Chapter Five.

23. *BCP*, 277.

24. I offer this observation, not only to show how the adoration of the cross continues the imitative pattern of identity formation, but to distinguish this ritual from schools of spirituality that have arisen within Christian history in which suffering tends to be glorifed and even pursued. See Herman-Emile Mertens, *Not the Cross, but the Crucified*, trans. by Gert Troch (Louvain: Peeters Press, 1990), 171.

25. *BCP*, 282.

26. See my exposition of Lathrop, p. 51 above.

27. *BCP*, 285.

28. The hotly contested debate among scholars about whether Jesus' final meal actually occurred on the Jewish Passover is irrelevant to the power that the transfiguration of Passover imagery comes to have for the early Christians. It is not the date of observance but the coherence and productivity of the paschal symbolism on its own merits that explains its liturgical prominence and enduring significance in Christian tradition.

29. Good treatments of the historical genesis of the elements of the Vigil liturgy can be found in Eigo, "The Easter Vigil."

30. *BCP*, 286.

31. "The Lord be with you...let us give thanks to the Lord our God...." It is note-

worthy that this exchange between deacon and people normally occurs as the beginning of the eucharistic Prayer of Thanksgiving. Louanne Bachner notes that the Exsultet is "consciously structured to read like a Eucharistic prayer...lacking only an institutional [sic] narrative and epiclesis." See Louanne Kathryn Bachner, "Fire, Story, Water, Feast: An Exploration of Liturgical Theology and the Poetics of Celebration in the Easter Vigil Liturgy," (diss., Emory University, 1990), 69.

32. *BCP*, 288; emphasis added.

33. Bachner, "Fire, Story, Water, Feast," 87–88.

34. Not all the lections are required, but the account of the deliverance of the people of Israel at the Red Sea is always included.

35. *BCP*, 288.

36. Alternatively, the liturgy may continue with the Epistle, Gospel, and Homily, and *then* the Baptism. I will address the ramifications of this discretionary choice in Chapter Six.

37. From the Thanksgiving over the Water; *BCP*, 306.

38. *BCP*, 302–303.

39. Ibid., 305–306.

40. Ibid., 306.

41. Ibid., 306–307.

42. Romans 6:3–4, 8.

43. Cf. Thomas Aquinas, *Summa Theologica*, III.73.3.

44. George Steiner, *Real Presences* (Chicago: University of Chicago, 1989), 231–232.

45. As my concern is with the liturgies of the American prayer book, I confine my reflection here to the western tradition. A very different, more mimetic liturgical treatment of Holy Saturday, compelling in its own way, is found in the eastern churches. For example, see Robert Taft, "In the Bridegroom's Absence: The Paschal Triduum in the Byzantine Church," in *La Celebrazione del Triduo Pasquale: Anamnesis and Mimesis* (Rome: Pontificio Ateneo S. Anselmo, 1990), 71–97.

46. Hans Urs von Balthasar, *Mysterium Paschale*, 2nd ed. (Edinburgh: T and T Clark, 1990), 168, 174–175.

47. Ibid., 176.

48. Hans Urs von Balthasar, *The Heart of the World*, trans. by Erasmo S. Leiva (San Francisco: Ignatius Press, 1979), 180–181.

49. Augustine, Sermon 272, in *The Works of St. Augustine*, Vol. III/7, trans. by Edmund Hill (New Rochelle: New City Press, 1993), 300–301.

50. William T. Cavanaugh, *Torture and Eucharist: Theology, Politics, and the Body of Christ* (Oxford: Blackwell, 1998), 229–230.

51. Louis-Marie Chauvet, *Symbol and Sacrament,* trans. by Patrick Madagan, S.J. and Madeleine Beaumont (Collegeville: Liturgical Press, 1995), 177.

52. Ibid., 177–178.

53. Robert Sokolowski, *Eucharistic Presence: A Theology of Disclosure* (Washington, D.C.: Catholic University of America, 1994), 195.

54. David Power, *The Eucharistic Mystery* (New York: Crossroad, 1994), 318.

55. Catherine Pickstock, *After Writing: On the Liturgical Consummation of Philosophy* (Oxford: Blackwell, 1998), 253ff.

56. Augustine, Sermon 354, in *The Works of St. Augustine,* 20. This way of speaking, as well as the citation in the footnote that follows, are the products of Augustine's interpretation of the prologue to the gospel of John.

57. Ibid., 21.

58. Ibid.

59. Ibid., 26.

60. Ibid., 26–27.

61. The mystical body of Christ and the church are not interchangeable in Augustine's thought, but the latter is, as it lives out the life it consumes in the eucharist, caught up in the former. See Eugene Portalie, S.J., *A Guide to the Thought of Saint Augustine* (Chicago: Henry Regnery, 1960), 257ff.

62. Augustine, Sermon 354, in *The Works of St. Augustine,* 27.

63. Augustine, Tractate 26, in *Tractates on the Gospel of John*, trans. by John Rettig (Washington, D.C.: Catholic University of America), 271.

64. Graham Ward, *Cities of God* (London: Routledge, 2000), 98.

65. Ibid., 100.

66. Ibid., 102.

67. Ibid., 105–106.

68. Ibid., 108–109.

69. Ibid., 112–113.

70. Robert L. Brawley, "*Anamnesis* and Absence in the Lord's Supper," in *Biblical Theology Bulletin* 20:4 (Winter 1990): 145.

71. The issue of presence and absence will reappear in Chapter Six, when we explore certain practical issues related to the celebration of Maundy Thursday.

72. The proper liturgies for Holy Week in the *Book of Common Prayer* are written in contemporary language. While for pastoral reasons they could be adapted to an older English form, this is done so rarely as to be hardly worthy of mention. Even so, the two prayers of the traditional language rite in the American prayer book are also West Syrian in structure. Here, I refer to the four prayers of Rite II—the contemporary language prayers—and to three new prayers in *Enriching Our Worship*, a supplemental manual of expansive-language prayers for use in Episcopal Churches with permission of the Bishop.

73. Hatchett, *Commentary*, 349–360; for a more detailed analysis, see Byron D. Stuhlman, *A Good and Joyful Thing: The Evolution of the Eucharistic Prayer* (New York: Church Publishing, 2000), esp. Introduction, chs. 3 and 8.

74. Early forms include the anaphora from Book 8 of the Apostolic Constitutions, the Liturgy of St. James, and the Byzantine Anaphora of St. Basil. In the American prayer book, Prayer D of Rite II is perhaps the fullest West Syrian prayer; based on a contemporary translation shared with several other denominations, this prayer is based on the third- or fourth-century Egyptian Anaphora of St. Basil.

75. In Chapter Five, we will give further consideration to the dynamic of anamnesis in the liturgical enactment of soteriology.

76. Eucharistic Prayer 2 from *Enriching Our Worship* (New York: Church Pension Fund, 1998), 61.

77. *BCP*, 306.

78. See Victor Turner, *The Forest of Symbols* (Ithaca: Cornell, 1967), esp. 93ff. His position is nuanced, but not fundamentally changed, in his more systematic and seminal work *The Ritual Process: Structure and Anti-Structure* (Ithaca: Cornell, 1969), esp. ch. 3. Behind his work lies that of Arnold van Gennep, *Rites of Passage*, trans. by Monika B. Vizedom and Gabrielle Caffe (Chicago: University of Chicago Press, 1960).

79. One wonders about the extent of influence of Hegelian philosophical categories on structuralist interpretations of ritual.

80. Rebecca Chop, "Foreword," in *Liturgy and the Moral Self: Humanity at Full Stretch Before God,* ed. by E. Byron Anderson and Bruce T. Morrill (Collegeville: Liturgical Press, 1998), x.

CHAPTER FIVE:

The Paschal Soteriology of the Triduum (II):
Liturgy as/and Soteriology

WE HAVE SEEN, in the preceding chapter, how the structural juxtaposition of the elements of the Triduum liturgies shape the liturgical assembly toward the assumption of Christ's own identity in remembrance, in priestly prayer for the world, anamnetic service, baptism, and eucharistic participation. This is the core of the Triduum's soteriology. We now revisit this paschal soteriology in two dimensions. First, we will explore the way in which the liturgy functions not as a reflection of salvation but as salvific act. This is the dimension of liturgy *as* soteriology. Second, we will characterize the soteriological "claims" of the Triduum, the ways in which it characterizes the redeemed life. Here we will attend to the connections between paschal soteriology and other areas of theological inquiry (ecclesiology, etc.), to the Triduum's counter-modern orientation toward suffering, and to the matter of human sin. We will also identify here one significant way in which this paschal soteriology adds to the conversation with other positions in the field of soteriology, especially in relation to the concept of sacrifice. We will conclude the chapter with a brief revisitation of the concerns of Jean-Francois Lyotard.

Paschal Liturgy as Soteriology

Any inquiry, in truth, starts in the middle. There is no other place to begin. In this inquiry, we have worked on the assumption that liturgy is not merely a decoration to the saved life but is the substantive enactment of it. This way of thinking about liturgy has allowed us to make some headway in understanding the change in the identity of the worshiping community over the course of time, from Ash Wednesday to Easter Sunday. It is now appropriate to step back from that assumption and say something about the warrant for thinking of the liturgy in this way and something about how liturgy works in this way.

Salvation has been rendered in many different ways in the Christian tradition, and in the Hebrew background from which it springs: release from bondage; imputation of righteouness; freedom; a quality of abundant life; forgiveness of sin; mystical illumination; gift of immortality; vindication at the Day of the Lord; and more. But the root of all these images is a relationship. Behind the complex of soteriological images lies the relation between God and humanity "in the garden" and the loss of it, whether that loss is construed as the understandable choice of an immature human not yet ready to choose well or a catastrophic fracture through disobedience, prompted by the devil. The deep logic of all soteriological images is relationship with God, regardless of the mode in which that relationship is described.

For Christians, this relationship between God and humanity is both revealed to us and lived for us in Christ. One might actually say, in fact, as Robert Taft has done, that the "liturgy of the new covenant is Jesus Christ":

According to the New Testament, it is this incarnate Lord and Savior in his self-giving, reconciling obedience to the will of the Father that for the followers of Jesus is the new liturgy. It is this, and not a new ritual system, that fulfills and replaces what went before: the new temple and its priest and sacrifice and victim; the new creation and the new Adam...the new Pasch and its Paschal Lamb— all are Jesus Christ in his saving life-for-others....[1]

Taft goes on to say, "Our liturgy, our service, is to be drawn into him, who is our incarnate salvation, and to live out his life, the same pattern he has exemplified for us...."[2] Our *liturgies*, in the narrow sense, are privileged places of entry into this paschal mystery, the lived and living disclosure of the life of God in Christ. As we enter into this life through Word and Sacrament, we enter into human wholeness. Again, Taft:

> The events of the past are the cause and mode of this reality's first manifestation or epiphany. But the salvific events of Jesus' earthly life, especially his dying and rising for our salvation, are more than just an epiphany or sign, more than just a manifestation of our salvation. They are the actual means of that salvation, its very instrumental cause.[3]

Into this reality we enter, not as "something outside of us which we contemplate, just as the dance has no subsistence apart from the dancers dancing, nor love apart from the lover loving the beloved."[4]

In worship, then, the assembly is in communion, in relation with God: in sound and silence, through listening and song, in praise and intercession; in lamentation and with thanksgiving, the people of God receive the gift of God's presence in Christ, hear God's judgment and call; and offer themselves to God through Christ's own self-offering. The lineaments of soteriology, then, are already here in the liturgy as the emergent worldview of the ritual relationship between God and humanity.

But how does this primary soteriology, this enactment of salvation come to pass? That is, from the assembly's side of this relationship, how does ritual *actualize* the paschal reality that emerges through its structural elements? In the case of the Triduum liturgies, how is it that the saving relation is enacted in these liturgies, rather than salvation being merely an idea or an object of mental assent, which could be called forth without ritual action? Furthermore, what is the relationship between the disposition of the participants and the power of the ritual as saving action? That is, what is the mode of their participation in this saving action? Finally, how does this salvation, enacted through the church's becoming Christ, maintain the fundamental commitment to the distinctiveness of Christ's saving work?

Anamnesis and the Formation of Ecclesial Identity

There are two aspects to the liturgical enactment of the saving relation that takes form in the paschal or Christic identity of the church. We might speak of these two aspects as *formal* and *dispositional*. The former has to do with how cultural and social identity is not merely expressed but is produced by ritual remembrance and how that memory becomes a habit of being. The latter has to do with the disposition of the participants—the conditions of faithful participation through which the Triduum liturgies can do their enactive work. The dispositional aspect of the ritual is dialectically constituted within the liturgy itself, and is reliant on divine grace from a point of view outside the liturgy. We will explain this in due time, but we turn first to the formal aspect of identity enactment that occurs in the Triduum liturgies primarily through their anamnetic quality. In his classic study on the bodily and performative aspect of social memory, Paul Connerton offers an extremely clear and succinct analysis of the role of ritual in bringing about a way of being in the world on the part of the participants. It is worth lingering over some of his observations as a way of understanding how the saving relation within the Triduum is enacted.

Connerton begins with the acknowledgement that "our experiences of the present largely depend upon our knowledge of the past" and that, in turn, "images of the past and recollected knowledge of the past…are conveyed and sustained by (more or less) ritual performances."[5] These performances take the form of commemorative ceremonies that produce habits of being that involve not only narrative retellings but "bodily automatisms."[6] Our knowledge of the past not only conditions our experience of the present but of the future. As if to confirm Metz's argument for a Christian experience of the "future in the memory of suffering"—an expectation of the future rooted in the *memoria passionis et resurrectionis*, in contrast to the modernist expectations of a future that can leave the past behind—Connerton argues that, in fact, the "world of the percipient, defined in terms of temporal experience, is an organized body of expectations based on recollection."[7] The commemorative ceremonies previously referred to are the vehicle for the communication of this social memory. People *become who they are*, in their experience of the world and their expectations of the future, through the narrative remembrance of the social body in which they ritually participate.

Connerton describes this process of becoming as the acquisition of habit. Habits of knowing and being occur, not by totally unconscious acts of driven behavior (addressed by psychoanalytic means), nor by "consciously applying to ourselves a rule of behavior,"[8] but by the nearly non-reflective way of living and behaving that arises from accumulative practice over time. The whole body of these (relatively) non-reflective, accumulated ways of being, seeing, and doing, as they characterize a people, amount to the social memory that shapes and organizes their world.[9] But how is this social memory communicated? By ritual practices, the "acts of transfer that make remembering in common possible."[10] Rituals are the pre-eminent case in which accumulative practice occurs.

How, then, do commemorative rituals work in creating the socially shared world that its participants *in-habit*? First of all, by contrast, ritual remembrance is not simply the symbolic expression of psychological experience prior to it. It is also more than the expression of textual or, by extension, conceptual notions already held.[11] Approaching rituals in this way limits their assessment to their content, assuming that the real point of the ritual is to express something "behind" the ritual practice and missing the very way in which not only their verbal expressions, but bodily repetitions, function to shape the participants' experience. By additional contrast, ritual is unlike the telling—or even acting out—of a myth, which has its power in that it can develop, change, and be told in a variety of ways, and leaves unspecified and open the particular relation between the participants and the events being told or acted. Ritual is formalized and marked by relative invariance, is thoroughly performative, and clearly specifies the relation between the performers of the rite and that which is being performed.[12] These are the modes through which ritual enacts, over time, a way of being in the world. Let us examine these features of ritual.

Ritual is formalized and performative. In liturgy or ritual, both the range of speech and bodily gesture is fairly defined (formalized). In contrast with the dramatic expression of myth, which can be done in a variety of ways, by many different authors, and through many creative means, there is a limited range of variation in ritual. Ritual is marked by the repetition of certain words and the inherited custom of bodily gesture that gives the liturgy its performative quality. Ritual speech does not have propositional or commentarial force, but is an action that brings about the state of affairs that it communicates.[13] "Blessed be God"…"We believe in one God"…"Almighty God have mercy on you, forgive you all your sins"…"Take, eat, this is my body which is give for you." All these highly regulated phrases, uttered in a context of shared intention, bring about in various ways the state, belief, or experience of reality to which they refer.[14] As Connerton states:

A blessing is no mere pious wish; it is understood to allocate fortune's gifts by the employment of words…. Curses, blessings, and oaths, together with other verbs frequently found in ritual language, as for instance 'to ask' or 'to pray' or 'to give thanks,' presuppose certain attitudes—of trust and veneration, of submission, contrition and gratitude—which come into effect at the moment when, by virtue of the enunciation of the sentence, the corresponding act takes place. Or better: that act takes place in and through the enunciation.[15]

The same effect holds by virtue of the plural pronominal language that dominates the ritual context. The regulated use of "we" and "us"—as in, "we give thanks" or "to celebrate the memorial of him who died for us"—constitutes the reality of a social community. Again, Connerton: "Prior to such pronominal utterance, there exists an undifferentiated preparedness, expressed by the presence of all the participants in the place where the liturgy is to be celebrated. Through the utterance of the "we" a basic disposition is given definitive form, is constituted, among the members of the liturgical community....In pronouncing the 'we' the participants meet not only in an externally definable space but in a kind of ideal space determined by their speech acts."[16]

The performative power of the liturgy to create, shape, and enact, rather than merely to refer to a state of affairs, is also a condition of the highly formalized use of bodily gesture. Kneeling, standing, the raising of hands in the *orans* position by the celebrant at the eucharist, receiving bread and wine in a prescribed fashion with outstretched hands, all possess a logic of their own that, over time, ingrain habits of knowing and being in the participants. The power of such performative action is not limited to the ritual occasion but permeates, indeed shapes and gives meaning, to the world of the ritual participant beyond the liturgical moment.[17] Connerton points out that much of this performative power arises from the limited range and spare repertoire of these bodily gestures. Contrasted with non-formalized communication, bodily or verbal, which can "be negotiated through a linguistic element of ambiguity, indeterminacy, and uncertainty," the spare range of possibilities in ritual gesture "strip communication clean of many hermeneutic puzzles" and "makes possible at once their performative power and their effectiveness as mnemonic systems."[18]

Ritual specifies the relation between the performer and that which is being performed. In raising the significance of this issue for ritual, Connerton again proceeds by contrast, in this case with the repetition of a dramatic work, or in the hearing of a musical piece recorded or performed once and then again. In each of these cases, the dramatic or musical performance stands as the complete expression of a musical or dramatic text, but the performance stands on its own. That is, a text written for performance only comes to life in that performance; the performance is the purpose of its writing and the repetition of the performances. They are instances of recurrence, but in an odd way; they do not repeat a founding text or document, but each is an instantiation of that text or document. Connerton observes, "…just as the repeated performance of the same play by different actors at different times accentuates the specific nature of each performance, and brings to our attention the differences between these performances, so also…the 'repeated' perception of the same text or recorded disc or film discloses the development of the perceiver's consciousness and brings to our attention the differences in each reading."[19]

The repetition involved in Christian liturgies, says Connerton, is something else again. Here, repetition or recurrence is tied to a founding act or text; what occurs here is a narration of salvation, through regulated gestural and verbal forms, that repeats the founding event in way that "actualizes" it anew without destroying the distance between the founding text and the liturgical performance, nor reducing the liturgy to mere mimesis of text or action totally external to it. For example, in the liturgical "rhetoric of re-enactment" of the eucharist, as Connerton describes it,

the celebrant is held to repeat once again that which Jesus Christ did, in giving again to the words which Christ used the same effi-

cacy which Christ gave them, by conferring on those words again
the power to do what they mean. There is…the primary performativity, by means of which Christ enabled certain words to do what
they meant. And there is, in addition, what we may call a secondary
or sacramental performativity, by virtue of which the celebrant, in
repeating these words in the context of the prayer of the canon, is
held to be restoring them to their primary performativity. In verbal
re-enactment of this kind we have embodied, not indeed total repetition, but the idea of total repetition.[20]

With this "idea of total repetition," Connerton offers us something
akin to the concept liturgists know as *anamnesis*, and brings home to our
study the import of his work to the rituals we are examining. In the liturgies of the Paschal Triduum, the enactment of the saving relation
between Christ and the people—a paschal identity of a church poured
out for the world *as Christ*—occurs through their anamnetic character.
The ritual repetition of gestures and bodily practices (footwashing,
kneeling prayers for all the needs of the world, washing with water) and
the enunciation of certain words in this doxological context ("Alleluia,
Christ is risen," "this is the night," "take, eat, this is my body," "Unite us
to your Son in his sacrifice,") actualizes or enacts the real relation
between the community and the Christ whom they serve. The identity
of the community, as agents of the same mission that Christ instituted,
emerges as the social identity of their constitution and this, in turn, is a
function of anamnesis, through which that constitution occurs, and
occurs again.

Consider again, for example, the act of the *mandatum* in the Maundy
Thursday liturgy. The invitation to the *mandatum* is, in the context of the
gospel and the prayer book anthems, not simply a reminder of Christ's
suffering service or an exhortation that servanthood is for whatever reason a good idea, but is a clear call to do this act in imitation of Christ. In

carrying this through—kneeling at the feet of others and washing their feet—the community inscribes the meaning of the present within the story of Jesus washing the feet of his disciples as a symbol of servanthood: this founding act is in tension with the present moment of the *mandatum*, while the present moment does, through gestural repetition and the context of verbal enunciation, bring this very servanthood to pass. Given the intention to participate, the *mandatum* becomes a powerful moment of communal transformation in which the people become Christ to one another. The *mandatum* has a secondary performativity that enacts or "actualizes" (in Connerton's terminology) this saving attitude or disposition toward the world, while never losing its diachronic tension with the primary performativity of the act of Christ that it repeats. Neither pure novum, nor mere mimesis of a past event, the anamnetic structure of ritual situates the footwashing as an enactive act that maintains its connection with its prototype. The relationship specified in ritual between the performer and that performed is neither mimesis, nor simple repetition, but anamnesis.

Consider as well the Exsultet, not as a gestural but a verbal example of anamnesis. The strange grammar of the Exsultet is anamnetic to its core. On the one hand, it recalls and repeats a prototypical event of the deliverance of the people of Israel from slavery in Egypt, through the Red Sea, to the promised land, and the deliverance of Christ from death and hell. Simultaneously, that recollection, uttered in a particular way ("This *is* the night, when Christ *broke* the bonds...") in the context of community gathered around the Paschal Candle, whose fire signifies the passing over of Christ from death to life, makes this community the delivered people at this moment, in this place. It does so by enacting the power of the original event, not by obliterating the original event or passing beyond it. The anamnetic Exsultet specifies and communicates a social memory of deliverance that now characterizes the present liturgical community. Over time, through repetition of this ritual action, and others deriving from it throughout the calendrical year that fleshes out the paschal observance, habits of confidence and a disposition of expectation that suffering is not the end will characterize the life of the community as they live in their present world. Yet, at no time is this communal *habitus* of saved existence disconnected from the prototypical events to which the anamnetic act makes reference.[21]

Connerton draws a firm contrast between the enactive repetition in ritual (which we are identifying as anamnetic) and the values of modernity. Connerton points out that modernity is characterized by a notion of progress, combined with a valorization of capital expansion: "...the essence of modernity is economic development, the vast transformation of society precipitated by the emergence of the capitalist world market. And capital accumulation, the ceaseless expansion of the commodity form through the market, requires the constant revolutionizing of production, the ceaseless transformation of the innovative into the obsolescent." The modern constellation of habits and attitudes cannot imagine "the possibility that there might exist forms of life that are exemplary because prototypical."[22] Connerton goes on to identify the "rhetoric of re-enactment" embodied in ritual practices as the way in which the imagination of an alternative—indeed, the alternative imagined—is cultivated. This is exactly the claim that we are making for the Triduum liturgies, not only in contrast to modernity, but in contrast to Lyotard and other post-modernists who mistakenly identify Christian practice with the modern metanarrative.[23]

The Disposition of the Participants in the Liturgy

If the saving relation between Christ and the church is enacted through the anamnetic performance of bodily practices and verbal enunications of the liturgical community, how is this affected by the disposition of the participants toward the liturgical action?

Let us return to Connerton's claim, quoted above, that "curses, blessings, and oaths, together with other verbs frequently found in ritual language, as for instance 'to ask' or 'to pray' or 'to give thanks,' presuppose
certain attitudes—of trust and veneration, of submission, contrition and
gratitude—which come into effect at the moment when, by virtue of the
enunciation of the sentence, the corresponding act takes place. Or better:
that act takes place in and through the enunciation."[24] Here, Connerton
names the dialectical structure of the disposition of the participants in
liturgy. On the one hand, the liturgy presumes a disposition of longing,
gratitude, and belief that brings the participants to it; on the other, the
longing, gratitude, and other affections of the heart and mind arise in the
participants as the experience of the liturgy and are brought into existence by it.

The liturgical enactment of the saving relation between participants
and Christ presumes a general level of intention on the part of those participants, however ambiguously or imperfectly focused, toward God's
action in the world as it is celebrated in the liturgy. With affectional
states of gratitude, longing, and faith, the participants come to the liturgy
seeking something that is often beyond naming, something that is no
more defined, perhaps, than that expressed in the catechumen's response
to the query, "What do you seek? Life in Christ." Some belief or provisional assent is also involved. On the other hand, the contours and character of the "Life in Christ" that they seek at life are often intuited but
not fully clear, because they emerge from the other side of the dialectic
of liturgical formation: the affections that the liturgy minimally presumes
for effective celebration are tutored, deepened, and in important ways
actually brought into being through the liturgical action itself. Beset by
the burdens of daily life and distracted by many things, participants come
with provisionally formed qualities of faith, expectation, and gratitude
that are given flesh through their practice as participants. The liturgy
cannot entirely "create" the dispositional conditions or beliefs that give

rise to effective enactment, but presumes some level of participant intention; at the same time, the dispositional orientation toward salvation
through Christ is dimly and imperfectly manifested in the hearts of those
who participate, and is stretched to full effect by the liturgical "practice"
of those dispositions and affections through which Christ works his salvation. The liturgy draws us out and gives shape to an intellective-affec-
tive orientation toward God. Don Saliers describes this dialectic as one
in which "the language of prayer…evokes and educates us in certain specific emotions by ascribing to God what is believed about God in the
vocative mode.…We are not merely referring to or naming emotions or
inner feelings. Quite the contrary, our attention and affective intention
targets God and, in so doing, it involves those deeper dimensions of the
human self expressed in the metaphor of the heart"—a metaphor by
which Saliers means all that we are, feel, and believe, "our capacities for
feeling and intending life at full strength."[25]

How does this dialectical quality of the dispositions of "the heart"
toward God avoid collapsing into a contradiction? What holds together
these provisionally formed dispositions of human persons with the specific dispositions shaped and learned in liturgy? The answer can only be
a claim of God's graceful working in the world, the very claim put in
motion by liturgical celebration. Although liturgy enacts a saving relation, it is not the liturgy that saves, but God through Christ. The very
celebration of liturgy in which human affections are schooled and dispositions formed already presumes the grace of God at work in the world,
wooing and drawing us into the worship of God. In the deepest sense,
the one liturgy is Jesus Christ himself, at work reconciling the world to
God as the very image of the nature of the abundant life in God. Our
liturgy, in the narrower sense—the liturgy of the Triduum, preemi-
nently—is an image of that image, as Robert Taft explains. This, says
Taft, is why the liturgical gathering is a "calling together," not a "coming
together." However distracted we are, however mixed our commitments,

however limited our desire, when we come to the liturgy with even this imperfect orientation of mind and heart toward God we do so because God is already at work in us. We are "saved" in this liturgical action as that orientation toward God is given shape, character, and depth by our "practice" of the paschal mystery in which all our suffering and our longing is made the doorway to abundant life. This is possible because God already knows that suffering and longing, knows the burden of mixed mind and divided heart, through the fully human life of the Christ who saves us. Having become like us to redeem us, he continues that work in the liturgical action in which we now become like him. Again, Taft: the purpose of the liturgy is "to turn you and me into the same reality [of Christ's saving work in the world]. The purpose of baptism is to make *us* cleansing waters and strengthening oil; the purpose of eucharist is not to change bread and wine, but to change you and me: through baptism and eucharist, it is *we* who are to become Christ for one another, and a sign to the world that is yet to hear his name."[26]

This brings us directly to the question of the distinctiveness of Christ's saving work, which must be addressed, given my insistence on the saving "fusion" between the identity of Christ and the church. If the liturgy is, first and foremost, Christ at work redeeming us for God, can we legitimately speak of ourselves as standing in the place of Christ for the world?

Possible Objections to the Present Approach

What I have referred to as the "fusion" of identity between Christ and the church through ritual action is crucial to the soteriological force of the liturgy. As we have seen, the people stand in the place of Christ in relation to the world, a relation initiated in the Maundy Thursday liturgy and coming to its most intense expression in the Good Friday liturgy. The people are thus prepared to celebrate the resurrection of Christ as their own transfigured life into which they enter, actually and proleptically. To enter into the place of Christ *is* to be saved, even in—precisely in—the midst of suffering.

One might object to this notion of the fusion of identity either as sacrilege (from a devotional point of view) or heresy (from a dogmatic point of view). Is it not the Christian affirmation, after all, that God, in the unfailing divine love, does for us in Christ what we cannot do for ourselves? That we trust in Christ for a salvation that comes from beyond us, and that the moral life we fashion is a response to this act of prevenient grace? With these questions in mind, some may argue that the fusion of identity that I find in the liturgy, through which the people become Christ to the world, is either mistaken or, if not mistaken, a justification for the continuing Protestant suspicion of liturgical worship!

To these potential challenges, I offer the following response. First, at the level of the content of the liturgy, the saving fusion of identity between Christ and the church is not pure or simplistic. The people continue, throughout the liturgy, to be receivers of and responders to Christ, as we have seen. There is a complex alternation between the first person and third person relationships between Christ and the church. This alternation is a dialectical dance within the ritual between thanking and beseeching God, on the one hand, and taking on Christ's pattern of behavior, on the other. What occurs in this dialectical dance, though, is that the people become God's answer to their own longing for salvation by their embodiment of the pattern of Jesus' life. This does not challenge the ultimacy of Jesus as Christ. Quite the contrary: it is, after all, *Jesus'* pattern of life that saves.

It may be helpful to borrow from the language of Louis Marie Chauvet to clarify this point. Chauvet, borrowing from Walter Kasper, observes that the resurrection of the crucified Jesus is the moment of conversion for humanity—the place where it becomes clear that Jesus was not put to death for his sin but that he died at the hands of ours. To the extent that our vision of ourselves is revolutionized by this resurrection, we ourselves are "implicated down to the very marrow of our desire." He goes on to say:

> A reversal of desire is demanded here, a reversal that would not only confess our own injustice in the very place where we arrogated to ourselves the authority—founded on our claim to be in the right, the right of "God's" very self—to condemn the just one, but also simultaneously confess a God completely other than our infantile desire's God of marvels, a God all the more easily manipulable "in good conscience" at the service of our ideologies....[27]

To recognize Jesus' as the example of how our own vision must be revolutionized is insufficient for our salvation as it leaves us in the position of knowing a new truth that can, once again, be turned into our own moral superiority, involving the very sense of disconnection from the other that allowed us to put Jesus to death in the first place. Mere solidarity with Jesus, on the other hand, can give rise to the same superiority to which we humans are inclined. Our salvation occurs at the intersection of exemplarity and solidarity. Recognizing the distinct difference of Jesus from us, by which we remain humbly aware of our inclinations to reject the other, we participate in the identity of Jesus. By this participation, we resist the human inclination to project our own ideologies onto others and turn away from the indifference to suffering and moral superiority that leads to our crucifixion of others.[28] Our salvation involves both our awareness of Jesus as an example and our patterning of our own lives on his life. It is this very dialectic between exemplarity and solidarity—between our recognition of Christ as the other in whom our brokenness becomes known and our desire for life exemplified and reoriented, and our assumption of his care for the other as the way in which that saving reorientation occurs—that is enacted in the liturgical oscillation between the first and the third person relations between Christ and the church. Far from being sacrilegious or heretical, the church takes on the identity of Jesus in liturgical enactment (solidarity) precisely as it renders thanks to God for this manifestation of the path to salvation that is revealed to us from the divine source beyond us (exemplarity), and because solidarity with that life even beyond the liturgy is the way to a full and whole human life.

Anamnesis, Epiclesis, and the Distinctiveness of Jesus Christ

Another way to approach the unitive tension between exemplarity and solidarity in the relation between Christ and the church is to return to the anamnetic character of this relation. In the anamnetic remembrance of Christ before God, we refigure the present by remembering the passion and resurrection of Christ that is, in Connerton's terminology again, its "prototype."[29] We remember the actions of Christ, not as a simple repetition, but with the self-conscious "idea of repetition" as the very content of the prayers and the purpose of the ritual action. In so doing, we refigure our lives around his saving pattern of suffering love, taking on his form of life, but do so with the conscious awareness of his life as the exemplar of this saving pattern. "His action is prior," as Taft observes, but we respond to the call by recapitulating that action as we remember the world before God, for example, in the Solemn Collects.[30] Always, we remember the world before God because God has first "remembered" us; that is, we are drawn into liturgical worship by the grace of Christ who, having lived our lives in consummate and full expression, remembers us still before God as our great High Priest.[31] God knows all of the heights and depths of human existence, even the extinction of death itself. Having known and lived this through Jesus Christ as the full and complete embodiment of such a human life, our own lives, with all their fractured intentions and mixed motivations, are brought to worship to be drawn into this paschal life of Christ, this one life lived to the fullest expression of God's purpose for the world. From this point of view, one must say that there is only one human life well-lived, and to the extent that we give ourselves to that life, liturgically and beyond, we are in complete solidarity or fusion with that life: we are Christ to the world, being *for the other*, because there is no other life to be lived.[32] At the same time, we live this life as a people called out by this One, and no other, whose life saves us all.

Another way to see the distance maintained between Christ and the church even in the heart of the soteriological fusion is to point out the relation between anamnesis and epiclesis. In the eucharistic prayer, we remember Christ's action through the words of institution and the *memoria passionis et resurrectionis*, and in that celebration, as we receive the Body and Blood broken and poured out, we become that body ourselves, broken for the world that Christ remembers still before God. We do so, however, through invocation of the Holy Spirit to make these gifts of bread and wine to be Christ for us, and to make the gathered community into Christ for the world. Even as we are united with Christ, we are aware that this unity comes as a gift of the Spirit whom God sends. The christic identity we have we do not own, because it is not a replacement of Christ in his work, but an extension and embodiment of it through a power given from beyond us.

In the Exsultet, or the Solemn Collects, one sees the same dynamic of the church's assumption of the paschal identity while, at the same time, recognition that this identity is given as a gift from Another who has gone this way before us. Even as the church exults in this night, the night in which we pass over from death to life in Christ, we recognize that the very power to sing the Exsultet comes from beyond. The song is a responsive act. The Solemn Collects, too, manifest this solidarity with the identity of Christ as the church becomes priest to the world as Christ was and is; yet it is to Another to whom they pray for that world, as that priestly identity flows from the "primary performativity" of Christ's own priesthood, into which they enter.

Paschal Liturgy and Soteriology

Christian soteriology involves critical reflection on the following: the human condition or human problem in relation to human destiny; the role of Christ in securing or transacting the solution to that problem or fulfillment of that destiny; and the way in which the human person appropriates that solution or goal. As such, soteriology is inextricably linked with other fields of inquiry—in particular, anthropology, christology, and ecclesiology. Eastern and western soteriologies typically work at the above-named issues in light of a cluster of biblical images, terms, and metaphors: creation/fall, sin, redemption, exodus/deliverance, sacrifice, healing, salvation, the reign of God, and the like. Some begin with an anthropology; others deduce anthropology from an organized pattern of several of the relevant biblical themes.

While every soteriology emphasizes one or another of these images and issues, there are predictable patterns that have emerged over time. Eastern Christian theology, linking the creation story and baptism to the philosophy of *exitus/reditus*, has settled into the theme of *theosis* as the most fundamental theoretical category within which to organize the various soteriological themes. Western soteriology has been more concerned with the biblical theme of sacrifice and the relation between law and gospel; consequently, the west has tended toward a focus on either the substitutionary or exemplary character of Christ's death on the cross and the translation of Pauline themes into doctrines of justification and sanctification—theories over which, regrettably, both ink and blood have been spilled.[33]

The soteriology of the Triduum, or any liturgical theology, is not "innocent" of theory. Anthropological assumptions and the emphasis on some biblical themes over others can be inferred from the structure and content of the liturgy in question. These are, however, emergent from the Christ-human relation enacted in the liturgy, rather than the liturgy being dramatic or mimetic illustrations of biblical themes of anthropological commitments. The method involved in doing theology this way assumes, again, that the liturgy is not simply words about God, but the enactment of world as God is drawing it into new being in Christ.[34] This is one thing that makes liturgical theology a distinctive and worthy conversation partner with other forms of soteriology that begin from different starting points, with a particular doctrine of God, notion of the fall, or anthropological construction. The soteriology of the Triduum "writes itself" in communal bodily practices that resist the modern sublimation of suffering. From the point of view of paschal soteriology, salvation is ethics, a "saving course of conduct."[35]

When we say that, within the nexus of the Triduum liturgies, salvation is ethics, this amounts to much more than the pedestrian, uninspiring, and finally unchristian claim that salvation comes from being "good," or even that salvation leads to moral action. The former claim is no more than a recapitulation of the idea that God loves us, or rewards us, because of our good works—an idea roundly condemned from the New Testament onward.[36] The latter claim is true, but it is true in the sense that action proceeds from character.[37] The deeper claim we are making here regards the form of life into which the Triduum shapes us—the *character* marked by self-offering love, servanthood, and a fearless attentiveness to the suffering of the world. To be drawn into relation, through worship, with Christ is to be drawn into a life marked by these things, and this life *is salvation*. Beneficial actions surely result—compassionate solidarity with the suffering—because they are both the content and the fruits of the formation, over time, of people who inhabit the world through a new way of being, a transformed character.

Given the internal relation among the Triduum liturgies, then, we must say that, for Christians, living life as loving servants to one another and to the world is not just the *path* to abundant life: it is itself the *char-*

acter of abundant life. Suffering will be an integral part of this life; unjust suffering will not be ignored, but named and challenged by this out-poured life; and this life may, in some case, lead to suffering and death as a consequence of its witness. In every cases, resurrection emerges in, through, and by the outpouring of life, honest to suffering, into which we are called and formed in the ritual action of the Triduum.

Paschal Soteriology and Sacrifice

The strong emphasis on the life of Christ in a paschal soteriology makes it an ideal conversation partner with current concerns over the concept of sacrifice. Some theologians, inspired by the work of René Girard, ques-tion whether the notion of sacrifice can escape inevitable connection with a doctrine of atonement as satisfaction for sin. Their concern with this linkage is that it tends toward a vision of God who transcendentally per-petuates the scapegoating mechanism, rather than undoing the horror of scapegoating, which they believe to be the real point of God's identifica-tion through the cross with the death of the innocent.[38] Other theolo-gians, for example certain feminist theologians, believe the sacrificial imagery of the cross is used to underwrite inappropriate, sometimes life-threatening sacrifices expected of women.[39]

Paschal soteriology recalls us to the reality that the sacrifice of the cross is not a call to masochism or self-abnegation. These are not identical with the servant identity. Furthermore, sacrifice does not refer only to the death of Jesus, as critics of sacrificial imagery sometimes assume. Sacrifice refers, first and foremost, to the pouring out of the divine life in love toward us and, second, to our response through participation in that life through Christ. Undertaking the work of Christ to service others who suffer will sometimes involve vigorous resistance to the causes of suffering, including scapegoating, oppression, and abuse. Jesus' own sacrificial life provides the model: he protected the adulteress from vindictive and unjust punishment and was never above excoriating the temple leaders for their contribution to the suffering of the poor.[40]

While a paschal soteriology offers this rejoinder to such concerns about sacrifice, it might accept a challenge as well: if this paschal soteriology emerges from liturgical action, are there ways in which the liturgical action works against its own logic? Certainly, the eucharistic prayers, within the Triduum, do not limit the sacrifice of Christ to a propitiatory death. Taken by themselves, however, the prayers do often reduce the sacrificial moral life of Jesus to a reference to his death on the cross. Many eucharistic prayers make no reference to the life of Jesus in the post-Sanctus, where it might most properly belong. This is a result of the assumption that the liturgical assembly is aware, from the whole range of practices of reading scripture, baptizing, and forming persons in faith, of the meaning of sacrifice as a description of a form of life. In the future, on the premise that liturgy contains the seeds of its own critique, we might safeguard against the misconstrual of this notion by drafting or expanding eucharistic prayers to make more explicit mention of the ethics of Jesus in the portion of the post-Sanctus concerned with him. An example of such a prayer currently in use is the second supplemental anaphora from *Enriching Our Worship*:

> Living among us, Jesus loved us. He broke bread with outcasts and sinners, healed the sick, and proclaimed good news to the poor. He yearned to draw all the world to himself, yet we were heedless of his call to walk in love. Then, the time came for him to complete upon the cross the sacrifice of his life, and to be glorified by you.[41]

The language of this prayer explicitly imagines the cross as the extension of Jesus' life, and not as a stand-alone, propitiatory act to an angry God or a symbol of masochistic self-denial. The insight that we are saved by Christ's whole life and death, and not by his death alone, is a real contribution of paschal soteriology to systematic soteriological projects and to future liturgical revision.

Paschal Soteriology and Other Theological Disciplines

More must be said about a paschal soteriology's construal of various forms of suffering. While this is our primary concern, we might extend beyond the core of this soteriology—characterization of the life of Jesus into which we enter by anamnetic participation—to attend briefly to ways that paschal soteriology could be worked out through other areas of theological inquiry. The full development of each of these areas awaits future work.

Historically, soteriology is a broad discipline. No single soteriology, either in substance or method, has ever attained orthodox status in the way that christology has done. In fact, soteriology can be a frustrating discipline because it seems to have to do with everything! At one time or another, soteriology has concerned itself with theological anthropology, christology, ecclesiology, moral theology, hamartiology, and the doctrines of the fall, grace, and last things. Here, we mention only ecclesiology, anthropology and the fall, and christology.

Ecclesiology

Because the church enacts its identity by gathering in the performative-enactive matrix of liturgy, and because the identity enacted there *is* the character of redeemed life, the relation between a liturgical soteriology and ecclesiology is very close. They are, in fact, two different ways of speaking of the same reality. Soteriology speaks of the creation and character of redeemed human life from the point of view of the ritual manner in which it is enacted; ecclesiology speaks of the redeemed life from the point of view of the corporate character and mission of the redeemed community in the world. One focuses on the redemption, the other on the redeemed community and its mission. The ecclesiology connnected to the paschal soteriology, then, foregrounds the biblical notion of the church as *the body of Christ* in the world. The church is a priestly people who intercedes for the world, attends to the suffering of the little ones, and models *relationship* above *product* as the salvation of a world caught up in the manipulation of information and technology in the pursuit of mastery over nature. However, this counter-witness to modernity is not tantamount to a sectarian vision. The life that the church models appears in every place and in every person where love and compassion are practiced in service to the deepening of human relationships. With regard to the church: the paschal life is practiced there, but not only there.

Anthropology and the Fall

Liturgical theology in general involves some anthropological assumptions: (1) Human beings are ritual beings, who come to their identity through the intentions incarnated in repetitive actions around symbols of life's deep sources. More precisely, those intentions are themselves the product of ritual action. Human beings come to be certain kinds of persons, in part, by repeatedly rehearsing in a regularized fashion certain values and perceptions in worship before God. (2) A corollary commitment is to the role of the body in the coming to be of the human person. In this anthropology, moral character is not simply expressed by bodily actions; rather, moral formation occurs through bodily action in which features of human character are rehearsed.

In this case, the overarching, redeeming human quality being bodily rehearsed in ritual is the quality of being-for-others. The implied human problem—both cause and result of the fall—is the pursuit of human flourishing as an individual affair in which the individual ego is fortified and defended against other human beings. The solution—the redeemed human life—is the opening of the self to the other. Human beings flourish, not as defended egos isolated from one another, but as servants of others, bodily involved, especially in the other's suffering and pain. The whole human person is one whose identity is found, counter-intuitively, by giving his or her life away, not as mere self-abnegation but as solidarity with other human beings in their growth, struggle and suffering. The anthropology at work in the enacted soteriology of the Triduum is a thoroughly relational one.

Closely related to the fall is the doctrine of sin. However, we shall defer remarks on sin until we have said more about the paschal soteriology's construal of human suffering.

Christology

Christology and soteriology have historically been entwined with one another: one focuses on the nature of Jesus Christ as divine-human relation, the other on the nature of that divine-human relation as saving for us. It is impossible to tease the two apart, as we would have no interest in the person of Christ if we were not laid hold of by the power of his life *for us*, nor could our attesting to that power emerge as anything other than a bone-deep conviction that the human and divine were ontologically in relation in him.

This being said, christology and soteriology can be *distinguished* in their focus, and there has been more contestation around the former than the latter. The ecumenical councils of the fourth and fifth centuries saw much debate over the proper way to speak of the person of Christ as divine and human, but that debate would not have arisen without the soteriological commitment shared on all sides that God was in Christ, saving us. Both Alexandrian and Antiochene emphases in christology— and the subtle variations of each in their mutual interactions—take seriously that Christ is God at work in the world. The paschal soteriology

enacted in the Triduum liturgies requires no particular allegiance to one
or the other christological approach, yet we offer the following two considerations.

First, according to the paschal soteriology of the Triduum, to live a life
open to all humans in their pain and suffering, and unafraid of our own,
is to enter into the very life of the One whose outpoured life is the mode
of being of the divine. In other words, to live as Christ is to enter into the
very life of God. This presumes a christology in which a true ontological
relation exists between God and Jesus the Christ, whose life is the pre-
eminent enactment of this abundant redemption. Any christology that
presumes an external relation between Jesus and God, in which Jesus is
called divine by virtue of his moral excellence, or in which he exemplifies
but does not participate truly in the divine life, would be an inadequate
partner to this liturgical soteriology.

Second, it may then be said that the language and content of the
prayers of the Triduum lean toward an Alexandrian or very high view of
the way in which Jesus Christ's relationship to God is construed. Christ
is not only "prayed through" but "prayed to" in collects, anthems, and
prayers in various parts of the Triduum.[42] On the other hand, neither the
appellation of "Son of God," nor the creedal affirmation that Jesus was
"conceived by the power of the Holy Spirit" rules out the emphasis of
the Antiochene theologians on the importance of the humanity of
Christ. Athanasius's christology, in which humanity is redeemed by
being caught up in the divine life of Jesus, runs the risk of making
humanity an abstraction from the concreteness of any particular life.[43]
The concern with the actual human life of Jesus, typical of theologies as
old as the Antiochene writers and as new as the liberation theologians,
must provide the content to christology. A paschal soteriology's impact
on christological construction keeps the life and behavior of Jesus
toward neighbor, stranger, disciples, and enemies in the forefront of the
imagination.

Paschal Soteriology and Suffering[44]

In the liturgies of the Paschal Triduum, the gathered community takes on
the identity of Christ as one who is open to the other and servant of the
other, not merely rehearsing this identity for some later action but enacting this identity already through prayer for the world and reverence for
the suffering of Jesus in which God's own service of the human other is
most fully realized. In the washing of feet, incorporation by water, prayer
for the world, and nourishment by the Body and Blood of Christ, the
church has begun to be a priestly people for the world as Christ was
priest for the world.

One of the things that distinguishes this paschal soteriology from the
classical soteriologies of the western tradition is that, despite the intentions of the latter to reconcile the divine and human in Christ, they sometimes harbor a logic of external relations between life of the Christian
community and the life of Christ. This is true of Anselm's theory, despite
its nuances and the sheer beauty of its symmetry, largely because of its
relentless emphasis on the incapacity of finite humanity before an infinite
debt of sin. Satisfaction theories of atonement are inclined to present the
appropriation of salvation as an act external to the believer, entailing a
cognitive or moral act by the beneficiary of salvation: accepting the salvation offered through Christ, one lives in response to this as Christ lived.
The problem here is that the moral character of Christian life stands
related to the life of Christ in an external fashion and, short of interven-
tionist views of the Spirit "helping" the Christian to live a life of appropriate moral character, there is little underpinning to the Christian life
other than the hope of salvation as an eventual external reward.
Exemplary theories of atonement, though focusing more on the suasive
and aesthetic power of the life of Jesus than on the crucifixion as a cosmic
transaction to right the offended order of the universe, still place the life
of Jesus and the life of the believer in a somewhat external relation to one

another.[45] The soteriology that emerges from the Triduum liturgies, however, is a participatory one: *salvation occurs, not as a final reward for living like
Jesus, but as part and parcel of the lived Christian life.* (The echoes of a
Johannine soteriology—the notion that eternal life begins here and now,
not after death—is not accidentally related to the use of the Johannine lections for Maundy Thursday and Good Friday.) Through the ritual practice
in which the church cultivates the sensibilities of Jesus and practices his
behavior, its members enter increasingly into the abundant life that he
knew. To enter into this life, one that was poured out in suffering and open
to those who suffer, *is* to be saved, made alive, made whole. The crucifixion and resurrection, the outpouring of life and the finding of it, are one
and the same indivisible moment in the celebration of the paschal mystery.

So then, three things might be said:

1. Salvation emerges through prayer, as Christians offer their
   hearts before God in love for the suffering world.
2. Salvation emerges as the embodiment of the priestly ethic of
   Christ, which is the identity into which the church enters
   through its prayer.
3. Salvation is prayerfully embodied as a clear-eyed reverence for
   the suffering of Christ as the fullest expression of his self-giving
   love for the world and the end to which he was led by his own
   fearless embrace of suffering human beings.

This last brings us squarely to the concern that animates this book. If,
from the liturgical-theological point of view, salvation is not simply cognitive assent or even grateful acceptance of something done on one's
behalf, nor an inspiring example worthy of eventual eternal reward if imi-
tated, but is the very form of life that constitutes the church, and through
which its members flourish as human beings, then what sort of people do
Christians become in relation to suffering? How does the ethic of salva-

tion enacted in the Triduum liturgies orient the Christian toward the suffering of human beings, in contrast to the Christianity Lyotard envisions and Metz challenges? Let us answer this question in the form of several suggestive theses that expand the logic of the Triduum's celebration of the life, death, and resurrection of Christ and ought to be taken into account in a full systematic soteriology. The reader is urged to recall the theological treatment of the Triduum, including the analysis of the structure of the eucharistic prayer, from Chapter Four.

Thesis One: God brings life through suffering.

Suffering is painful and unromantic, but it is not the end of all hope; to the contrary, "the way of the cross is the way of life." In the Triduum liturgies, the new and transfigured life into which Jesus was resurrected happens not as an afterthought, a happy ending, or a mere vindication of his teaching. Maundy Thursday and Good Friday draw the participant into his suffering because God enters into it and makes it life-giving. The Easter liturgy celebrates that life by baptizing new members into his death and sharing table fellowship around the story of his suffering. Suffering is no less painful, but is less to be feared, because it is revealed to be a constitutive feature of the outpoured life through which God is present to us. Rather than fleeing from suffering, Christians are formed into a people attentive to suffering as a mystery in which God is at work.

This much, we have seen. But can something more be said of the implications of a paschal soteriology for various kinds of suffering?

Thesis Two: In the Triduum, suffering of every kind is caught up in the cross as the field of redemption and the matrix of resurrection.

Some have seen the suffering of the cross as a particular kind of suffering: either unjust suffering imposed by the religious and civil authorities of Jesus' time, or suffering that Jesus undergoes to "take our place" under the wrath of God, as thin versions of Anselmian soteriology will sometimes claim.[46] This can have several infelicitous effects for a theological account of suffering. It can leave some forms of suffering—for example, the griefs small and large that are endemic to human growth and development—outside of Christ's self-giving life that culminated in the cross. To connect the God of Jesus Christ to these griefs would require additional steps of a general account of God's compassion that may not be adequately connected to Calvary. Alternatively, it can connect the gospel of salvation to a concern with only one kind of suffering, turning the "preferential option for the poor" into a divine exclusivism. A third alternative is that it can sidestep the reality of suffering altogether by accounting it "just," that is, the suffering of the cross is necessary to satisfy God's justice.

It is true that in the Triduum the immediate account of suffering is that which is the culmination of the religious and civil authorities to Jesus. Yet, this culmination is the end of a life of outpoured love that came to be in the same way our own lives do. Jesus' identity as one-for-others, the servant of all and especially the broken and the outsider, came to fruition over the course of a life. He grew from childhood to adulthood and can only have suffered the normal pangs of self-differentiation and the struggle to understand himself. He had to have known the death of friends and loved ones as well as birth, sorrow, and loss as well as joy. He wrestled with his vocation as we do, spending long hours of time in prayer and meditation alone as he came to grips with his identity. Even at the last, in Gethsemane, he struggled for clarity on the right course of action, yielding ultimately to God's will. This is the life every human being lives; we might say, more truthfully, that in him every human being lives this life. In the liturgies of the Triduum, the suffering of Christ is not caused by unjust political power or an instance of human moral intransigence alone, though it is clear from the dense description of the gospels that self-interested political machination and repressive power is at play. Rather, the crucifixion is held up as consistent with the whole of Jesus' identity expressed in his ministry of compassion and service, an identity that came to be through all the losses and joys of life. This is why Christian popular devotion has often found comfort in the cross for the everyday suffering of our lives. This is why the church prays in the Solemn Collects not only for church and government but for "the hungry and the homeless, the destitute and the oppressed...the sick, the wounded and the crippled...those in loneliness, fear, and anguish... those who face temptation, doubt and despair...the sorrowful and bereaved...[and] for prisoners and captives and those in mortal danger."[47] In the liturgies of the Triduum, all suffering—psychodynamic, physical, emotional, spiritual, economic, political, the suffering that is actively chosen and the suffering that follows from the coming-to-be of human identity—is drawn into the hope of redemption and becomes the doorway to it. Christ enters into our full humanity and draws it all into the saving action of his life of outpoured love.

Thesis Three: God redeems all our suffering; but not all suffering demands the same response.

One might object that this paschal soteriology risks quietism in the face of the suffering that is inflicted on human beings by others. By bundling all suffering into the cross and declaring that God's redemption is there, do we not valorize suffering? More precisely, does the Triduum dull our capacity for response to the suffering caused by political oppression and the fearful use of authority because God works redemption through our suffering? Would not the soteriology of liberation theologies do better in squaring the fact of the cross with Jesus' witness for the poor and oppressed?

Given that all human suffering is caught up in the suffering of Christ, every instance of human suffering is worthy of the attentive care of a priestly people. But every form of suffering is different, and is felt by the sufferer each in her own way. Being Christ to others in their suffering requires, at times, the willingness to face our own suffering and learn from it; at times, it requires the courage to sit with others in their suffering; and at other times, it requires our efforts to alleviate or resist the suffering at hand. The psychodynamic suffering that arises from the struggle to come into one's identity, for example, and the suffering of the political prisoner are two very different kinds of suffering. The ability to discern the difference and the courage to respond appropriately, as Jesus did, are cultivated over time by the internalization of the sensibilities of Jesus in the liturgical action of the church as it hears and responds to the whole range of Scripture throughout the liturgical year.[48] During that year, the liturgical assembly sees Jesus at times showing compassion to those who suffer and, at other times, challenging those who cause suffering. While the Triduum liturgies are the high point of the year, they are not isolated: they are, to adapt *Lumen gentium*'s language for the eucharist, the source and summit of the Christian year. The differentiation among the woes of human beings and our capacity for differentiated response is demonstrated through the gospels and echoes in the Triduum worship.

One recalls, too, that the Triduum liturgies celebrate the life of one whose *own* suffering arose, in part, as a result of his solidarity with *others* who suffered by their forcible exclusion, oppression, and mistreatment. That is precisely *how* God is present to those who suffer injustice: Christ, and now the church as his body, pour out their own lives to help and strengthen those who suffer, including those who suffer unjustly. But this priestly ministry cannot be done by those who will not first acknowledge such suffering, or who turn away form it with the naïve tolerance of the modernist that, unpleasant as it is, it finally does not figure into the history of capital expansion and technical mastery that will ultimately eliminate it.

Thesis Four: Christian faith as enacted in the Triduum does not valorize suffering for its own sake, but knows God is present even there.

The paschal soteriology does not valorize suffering. The key to the distinction is in the Maundy Thursday and Good Friday liturgies each of which, in the ways we have seen, make the focus of ecclesial identity not the suffering of the cross as such, but the person whose manner of life is symbolized by the cross on which his physical life was ended. As Herman-Emiel Mertens stresses in his choice of title for an essay on soteriology, it is "not the cross but the crucified" that is the church's focus. It is the crucified and risen one whose manner of life the church makes its focus as it becomes, in extension of his life, Christ to the world.

This distinction is important, not only because of the need to resist a false theology that might glamorize suffering to the point of reducing our resistance to the suffering that can and should be alleviated—for example, the suffering of the economically poor or political prisoners—but also because the focus on the crucified keeps the focus on the ethics of Triduum faith. As Mertens says:

> Undoubtedly, faith in the Crucified One is a "*cross*-faith." Yet every attempt to erect an ideology of the cross should be radically rejected. A Christian neither looks for the cross, nor chooses to die. Every form of dolorism or extreme asceticism is to be avoided. Self-castigation is pure masochism (it may even reflect a too competitive spirit, or haughtiness). "Not the cross, but the Crucified" is our hope....Well understood, "cross-faith" does not at all affect the lust for life. But it surely illuminates the evangelical paradox that "whosoever loses his life...will save it" (Mark 8:35).[49]

Not the cross, but Jesus' life, with which his death on the cross was completely consistent, fleshes out the ethics of salvation for the church.

Thesis Five: Even in the Coming Reign of God, suffering and those who suf-fer are not forgotten.

One of the primary biblical symbols of salvation is the kingdom or reign of God. This symbol dominates the teaching of Jesus in the synoptic gospels and remains important even in the gospel of John, which is more didactic and less parabolic. In this image, one sees the connection between the growth of the cosmos and the process of character develop-ment in the human person. Both take *time*, which liturgy sanctifies (along with space) as the field of God's activity among us. But the sym-bol of the eschaton or reign of God is one of completion, in which time ceases and God's purpose is brought fully to pass. Suffering, which is inextricably connected to the "motion" of time,[50] is said to be relieved in the eschaton, when God "will wipe away every tear."

But the memory of suffering does not cease, because it is in the suf-fering of the crucified that the risen life of the kingdom comes about. Thus, while the Book of Revelation speaks of the wiping away of every tear, it credits this consummation of human suffering to the one on the throne: the Lamb *that was slain*.[51] Here, the imagery of the passover—the pasch—remains in the forefront. Given the paschal mystery—the mystery of abundant life emerging in, through, and by Christ's suffer-ing—whatever is meant by the coming reign of God, it cannot involve the forgetfulness or overcoming of suffering in any simplistic way. The repression of a whole dimension of created existence yields a thin version of the reign of God.

This truth, expressed in the Book of Revelation, appears in many apocryphal and hagiographic stories in which the risen Christ is known by the scars of his passion. (For example, recall the legend of Martin of Tours who, when visited by a glorious figure in a vision who claimed to be Jesus, asked the figure to show Martin the scars on his body. The fig-ure disappeared, it is said, and Martin knew he had been visited by the devil.) These eschatological images make it impossible to envision the consummation of all things without remembrance of the suffering of all creation that was embraced by God's Son in the outpouring of his own life that makes this consummation possible. Such a vision of the eschaton, rehearsed in the liturgies of the Paschal Triduum and spilling over into Christian life within the world, alone offers a challenge to the modernist diminishment of human experience. In the Triduum liturgies is the flashpoint where the imagination of reign of God and the practice of the remembrance of suffering come together in the formation of a people as Christ to the world, in solidarity with all who suffer.

Paschal Soteriology and Sin

The theses I have sketched are only the beginning of a full, systematic soteriology. Some, however, will already question either the usefulness or the orthodoxy of paschal soteriology since, while it is concerned with sin, sin is not its *sole* concern. The Triduum liturgies themselves make abundant reference to sin. Yet, those references occur alongside reference to a cluster of human maladies that are not traced solely to sin in the language of the rites. The Maundy Thursday liturgy concerns itself almost entirely with the themes of love and servanthood; the celebrant's bidding at the Great Vigil of Easter makes no mention of sin, but of "the Passover of the Lord, in which, by hearing his Word and celebrating his sacraments, we share in his victory over death."[52] That liturgy turns to sin references for the first time in the Exsultet. This is not at all to suggest that the Triduum is unconcerned with sin, but that the sweep of its concern is broad and does not identify the human problem as only a matter of disobedience. This mirrors the rich soteriological tradition of Christianity in which the relationship between immortality and mortality, the human will, human disobedience or sin, and the devil's deception are construed in many different ways.

Still, there are those who would argue that the saving work of Christ aims primarily at the forgiveness of the sinner, and suggest that doctrines of propitiation or satisfaction are properly the cardinal Christian soteriology. Such critics will find the paschal soteriology I sketch here unsatisfactory. In fact, propitiatory doctrines have a foundation in the Scripture, as do most other soteriologies as well. But the notion of propitiation for sin alone is an inadequate and uninspiring soteriological model for our day. It is inadequate because of limitation to a particular form of human suffering, that of the pain and consequences of sin. A paschal soteriology emerges from the dense liturgical narrative in which sin certainly comes to the foreground as the cause of Jesus' death. Jesus could take up human sin as one of the dimensions of human existence and struggle because he, above all, felt the impact and consequence of sin in the form of his own rejection and sacrifice to the fear of love and self-service. In short, he knew the ravages of human sin even if, as the traditional formulation has it, he himself did not sin against others.[53]

In our own context, much from the result of our psychological sophistication, we are acutely aware of the unavoidable depth of human suffering that ranges far beyond that which arises as a consequence of sin. Christ's own "remembering" of the world before God by taking on all of humanity in himself did not overlook sin, but was not restricted to it either. The Athanasian principle applies here: "that which is not assumed is not redeemed." If we are to be redeemed from all that we suffer, then Christ must have taken on all that we suffer. This is exactly the soteriology of the Triduum liturgies: they present the cross not only as the outcome of sinful human behavior, but as the symbol—indeed, the very nature—of Christ's entire life and as the way in which he entered into the fullness of humanity, its struggles and losses. A soteriology that witnesses to Christ reconciling sinners to God as the totality of his saving work fails the Athanasian completeness celebrated in the Triduum liturgies: Christ's entry into *all* human suffering, not simply that of sin. It does not follow from this broad concern with suffering that sin is excluded, only that soteriology is not restricted in its concern to sin alone.

Yet, one might press: does not the Genesis account itself make clear that the human problem is one of sin, and that all suffering flows from this? Perhaps. However, even if one grants the strongest possible argument for sin as the root cause of all other suffering, still a soteriology that deals with sin alone is insufficient in accounting for this other suffering and God's remedy to it. Demonstrably, the forgiveness of our sin, for which one surely gives thanks, does not relieve us of struggle and suffering in life. As pivotal as it is, this account must also be seen as testimony to the larger sweep of our struggle and longing. Granted, the Genesis account suggests that the sin of Adam and Eve led to the struggle of humanity beyond the gates of Eden, a life in which all accomplishment comes hard and only with the cost of worry and labor over every small gain. But, the Genesis account, however important, is not the first and last word on the human problem. The Bible also speaks to the reality that all suffer the vagaries of time and chance. The psalms and wisdom literature are replete with the voice of lamentation arising from unjust oppression, illness, depression, and the sheer toughness of human life. Jesus himself says that the rain falls on the just and the unjust, and exhibits little patience with the notion that all suffering can be reduced to human sin.[54] In the Triduum, we enter into the deep mystery that we have always suffered and struggled. These have always been with us: the mental anguish of deciding among competing critical goods in a world tragically structured by finitude;[55] the pain of the death of dreams and unrealized hopes; the loss of innocence as we grow into the knowledge that those who have brought us into the world we inhabit are no less confounded by its hidden traps than we are; the outrage and loss at the death of an innocent child; and surely enough, the pain of injustice and the wounds of sin. God must heal us here or not at all, and we must go before God with the open acceptance of this reality of our suffering, because that is precisely where we are met by God. This is the one condition, the root requirement, by which the power celebrated in the liturgies of the Triduum can set us free, right in the midst of things as they are. If Christian soteriology at least since Anselm has been almost exclusively concerned with sin, it is now time to draw both from the deep logic of the Triduum and the whole breadth of Scripture a soteriology that speaks to all human travail.

"This is the night, when you brought our ancestors out of bondage in Egypt, and led them through the Red Sea on dry land....This is the night..." This is the night, and now is the time, as we remember Christ who remembered us, entering into the suffering, pain, and loss of human life and taking it up as a high priest before God, transfiguring our suffering and breaking it open to reveal the undefeatable love of God. This is the night, and now is the time, when we dive down deep into the suffering of the world, take it up into our own lives as Christ to those around us, and emerge a new people to find our own suffering transformed as well. This is the gift of salvation from God, brought to be in Christ, performed in the Triduum and practiced beyond it, honest to the human condition, and full of hope in the midst of sorrow, including our sorrow at our sin. It is this great paschal mystery by which we live.

A Final Note: Responding to Lyotard

From the standpoint of paschal soteriology, what sort of response can one make to Jean Francois Lyotard? It is clear, beyond the question of the theological heart of Christianity, that Christians are no less subject to the pressures of modernity than anyone else. It is equally clear that Christianity, an Incarnational faith that reveres the created order and the best of the human world, has at certain times and in certain places become entangled with the less salutary values of its cultural context.

One might argue that Lyotard has misunderstood the *type* of narrative that is the Christian faith. Lyotard claims that narratives have a lethal function with respect to the past. This lethal function is critical to the totalizing power of narrative, as it eliminates any ground from which the present must answer. The totalizing narrative can thus completely inscribe the experience of the hearer without remainder as it is oriented entirely toward the "act of recitation" of the narrative. Connerton has argued, however, this is the function of mythic narratives. One might argue that Connerton's work implies a different *type* of narrative—anamnetic narrative—and claim that Lyotard has simply not understood the various genres of narrative, not all of which function in the same way. It is true, after all, that the Christian narrative, as anamnetic, constitutes an identity in the present, through the epiclesis of the Spirit of Christ, that is drawn from the past as a prototype. This, again, is why the verbal enunciations and gestural actions are spare, relatively limited, and highly regulated: they are meant both to establish the character of present reality and circumscribe it within a past in which the true character of the human constantly stands to critique, inspire, correct, and animate the present, through the invocation of help from beyond.

A truly theological response to Lyotard must go farther, however. It cannot argue over the philosophical character of narratives only, but from the shape of the life enacted in the liturgy and lived beyond it. Unless it attempts to work by canons external to it, Christian theology must respond to Lyotard on its own terms. There is no substitute for witness and no guarantees but God's grace that such a witness will be possible in the liturgical assembly's life in the world. Liturgy is not a machine, and Christian formation is not automatic, or the result of a formula.

To clarify, we might review the methodological character of the liturgical theology that we have outlined. Liturgical theology begins from the structural juxtapositions of ritual action and gives voice to the meaning enacted by the congregation through those structures. Its primary data is this ritual action and the relationship that it brings to pass between God's action in Christ and the character of the liturgical community. I have argued that all of life is there in that enactment of the Triduum liturgies: at our best (by the grace of God), we remember and attend to the suffering of humanity before God because, through that liturgical action, we enter into Christ's own life as high priest for the world. Christ's action is prior: we remember the world in its suffering, and offer our own to God, because Christ has first remembered us before God. Our remembrance of suffering and entry into life as a priestly people is an entry into salvation because it is Christ's life into which we enter, and by which we have access to God's being in the suffering world. More precisely, because Jesus is the Christ, *the world's suffering is already taken up into the divine life.* This is, as Christians confess, a fact. To be priests to the world is to join with Christ in that taking-up of suffering into the heart of God.

One does well to return to Robert Taft on this point, who argues that "the liturgy of the New Covenant is Jesus Christ," and that "our liturgy, our service, is to be drawn into him, who is our incarnate salvation, and to live out his life....In short, our salvation is God's glorification, and he gives it to us, not we to him. He does this through his Spirit dwelling and moving in his church." Our liturgies, in the sense of our ritual practices, are the avenues (though not the only avenues) through which we enter into this salvation and participate in his life.[56]

Methodologically speaking, this means that liturgical theology does not proceed as an apologetic theology in the traditional sense, attempting to correlate the images and metaphors of Christian faith to the experience of human suffering. It proceeds, rather, as a "second-order redescription" of the way in which the church lives, and what it proclaims, in its liturgical action.[57] The church is judged by that life. The Christian narrative enacted in the liturgy is the performative expression of that life as it is saved and redeemed by God.

The Christian narrative itself is given its character and structure by the gracious participation of God in our suffering, such that our suffering is taken up into the divine life. The narrative is formed by the character of God's saving action, not the contrary: God breaks into history and gathers up the suffering and brokenness of the human and transfigures it, dwelling there and making it into the doorway to the divine life. In worship, the people of God enter into that action, and as both witness to that enactment and the way in which it is enacted, a story is told, marked by the *aporias* and displacements of time that point beyond themselves to the embrace of the human by the God beyond time and place. The narrative Christians "tell," in word and bodily practice, is one that undoes our commitment to the tidiness of technical and capital progress by making us attentive to suffering, offering our own and the world's to God as a priestly people. If this is what God is up to in the world, then the theological response to Lyotard can only be a performative one. It does not proceed by rearranging, altering, or defending the Christian narrative in philosophical argument, but in living the Christian life and calling others to it.

To be fair, Lyotard has some warrant for his treatment of the Christian narrative as an abstract master story of history since Christians themselves, throughout the Constantinian period, have treated the Christian narrative as if it were a grand explanatory narrative of human history.[58] It is perhaps not unrelated that the practice of the Triduum began its long demise in this same period, being recovered only recently as liturgical revisions were made in the light of a modernity under suspicion, scarred by world wars and an awareness of the modern capacity for genocide. With the recovery of the Triduum, set within the late modern recovery of the importance of symbolic ritual to human character development, the church has re-entered a process of moral formation that may yet draw us into the witness for which Metz hoped.

It is Metz, we recall, who is concerned that the modern theologies fail to distinguish between "the negativity of suffering and the negativity of

the dialectically mediated concept of suffering."[59] A theory of suffering
as an abstraction fails to honor theologically the concrete pain and
struggle of human life, in the same way that Lyotard's theory of narrative
fails to honor the concrete power of narrative that testifies to a human life
not distanced from concrete suffering, but more attentive to it. In the
liturgical practice of theology, however, the anamnesis of the Triduum
lifts up and names the very real suffering, longing, and pain of the participants and of the world. That real struggle is caught up in the narrative enactment, through the three days, of a living story of priestly
mission that carries the church into a future of hope. Contrary to the
modernist abstraction of the future whose *telos* requires suffering to be
repressed or wished away, the Triduum liturgies shape a church whose
future emerges from the narrated eucharistic memory of the suffering of
Jesus Christ as the suffering of all humanity, and the presence of God in
all human suffering.[60] What is left to Christians is the faith that God will
not give up on our failures to live the life of Christ and will draw us again
to prayer and to witness.

Notes

1. Robert Taft, "What Does Liturgy Do? Toward a Soteriology of Liturgical
Celebration: Some Theses," in *Primary Sources of Liturgical Theology*, ed. by Dwight
W. Vogel (Collegeville: Liturgical Press, 2000), 140.

2. Ibid.

3. Ibid., 142.

4. Ibid.

5. Paul Connerton, *How Societies Remember* (Cambridge: Cambridge University
Press, 1989), 3–4.

6. Ibid., 5.

7. Ibid., 6.

8. Ibid., 25–29, 34. Connerton is here quoting Michael Oakeshott, *Rationalism
in Politics* (London: Methuen 1962), 119–129.

9 Cf. Thomas Aquinas's treatment of dispositions and virtues. See Thomas Aquinas, *Summa Theologica: A Concise Translation,* ed. by Timothy McDermott (Westminster, Md.: Christian Classics, 1989), 224ff.

10. Connerton, *How Societies Remember,* 39.

11. Ibid., 44–50.

12. Ibid., 53–57.

13. Ibid., 57–58.

14. By "shared intention" I mean that these utterances have force for those who intend, at whatever level of strength, to participate in the liturgy, as opposed to someone who might be observing its practice for descriptive purposes. This relates to the question of the dispositional conditions for authentic liturgy to which we will attend below.

15. Ibid., 58.

16. Ibid., 59.

17. Ibid., 44.

18. Ibid., 59.

19. Ibid., 67.

20. Ibid., 68; Cf. Pickstock's "non-identical repition," *After Writing,* 109, 160.

21. Both the *mandatum* and the Exsultet (uttered at the conclusion of the "passage" of the people into the sacred space from the lighting of the New Fire) are mimetic events, as are the eucharist or the many other anamnetic elements of the paschal liturgies. Anamnesis always involves a mimetic foundation, as its connection to the founding event or "prototype" of the celebration; anamnesis is larger than mimesis however, transforming mimetic act and word, in the formalized context of liturgy, into a performative creation of present reality. For a related note on this relation between anamnesis and mimesis, see Barbara DeConcini, *Narrative Remembering* (Lanham: University Press of America, 1990), 63.

22. Connerton, *How Societies Remember,* 64.

23. We return to this on p. 131, below.

24. Cf. Kavanagh's comment on liturgical enactment, pp. 33 and 112, above.

25. Don Saliers, *The Soul in Paraphrase: Prayer and the Religious Affections,* 2nd. ed. (Cleveland: OSL, 1991), 18, 24ff.

26. Taft, "What Does Liturgy Do?," 144.

27. Louis-Marie Chauvet, *Symbol and Sacrament* (Collegeville: Liturgical Press, 1995), 501.

28. Ibid., 501–507.

29. See the discussion of Connerton, 102ff.

30. Taft, "What Does Liturgy Do?," 140.

31. One recalls, here, the strong priestly themes that make up the fabric of the Triduum liturgies, and the explicit reference made in that regard by the reading from the book of Hebrews on Good Friday.

32. Note the relation of this claim to Karl Barth's famously peculiar claim of the "ontological impossibility of sin" and its connection to his christology. See Barth, *Church Dogmatics*, vol. 3/2, ed. by G. W. Bromiley and and T. F. Torrance (Edinburgh: T & T Clark, 1960), 132ff.

33. There are important differences among the western soteriologies of, for example, Augustine, Anselm, Abelard, and Thomas Aquinas, not to mention the contemporary theories of Tillich, Moltmann, the feminists, et al. Others treat these differences in detail: see John McIntyre, *The Shape of Soteriology* (Edinburgh: T & T Clark, 1992); Herman-Emiel Mertens, *Not the Cross But the Crucified* (Louvain: Peeters Press, 1992). My purpose here is to provide a context within their family resemblance to identify what is distinctive about a soteriology sketched as a liturgical theology.

34. Kavanagh, *On Liturgical Theology*, 168.

35. The phrase is that of Clement of Alexandria, *Paedagogos* (New York: Fathers of the Church, Inc., 1954), Book I, ch. 7.

36. Romans 4:1ff.

37. John 15:4–5; Romans 12. Here I am closer to the Thomistic position on the relation between faith and the moral life, than to the Reformers' view. For example, Cranmer's view on the "annexation" of good works to faith, or Luther's sharp distinction between salvation and holiness, are not adequate to the complex and organic relationship between salvation and ethics in liturgical action. Cf. Thomas Cranmer's "Homily of Salvation" and "Homily of Good Works" in *Miscellaneous Writings and Letters of Thomas Cranmer* (Cambridge: Cambridge University, 1846), 128–134, 141–149; and Martin Luther, "Confession Concerning Christ's Supper," in *Martin Luther's Basic Theological Writings*, ed. by Timothy F. Lull (Minneapolis: Fortress Press, 1989), 50–62.

38. Various ways of addressing the problem Girard proposes can be found in J. Denny Weaver, *The Nonviolent Atonement* (Grand Rapids: Eerdmans, 2001); James Alison, *The Joy of Being Wrong: Original Sin Through Easter Eyes* (New York:

Crossroad, 1998); Anthony W. Bartlett, *Cross Purposes: The Violent Grammar of Christian Atonement* (Harrisburg: Trinity Press, 2001).

39. Rita Nakashima Brock and Rebecca Ann Parker, *Proverbs of Ashes: Violence, Redemptive Suffering, and the Search for What Saves Us* (Boston: Beacon Press, 2001).

40. An excellent account of the meaning of sacrifice in Christian theology and the eucharist is offered by Rowan Williams, *Eucharistic Sacrifice: The Roots of a Metaphor* (Bramcote, Notts.: Grove Books, 1982). See also S. W. Sykes, *Sacrifice and Redemption: Durham Essays in Theology* (Cambridge: Cambridge University Press, 1991).

41. *Enriching Our Worship*, 61.

42. The early history of christology is complex, including the subtle interactions of Alexandrian and West Syrian theologies. No attempt is being made to simplify that complexity here. For example, Origen argues, despite his Alexandrian provenance, that our prayers are to be offered through Christ, although the later Alexandrian position takes much "higher" position. (See Origen's *Treatise on Prayer*, in *Alexandrian Christianity*, ed. by Henry Chadwick [Philadelphia: Westminster Press, 1954], sects. 15.1–16.1, 269–271.) At the same time, Origen's position is echoed in the early form of Antiochene eucharistic prayers such as the one found in the eighth chapter of the *Apostolic Constitutions*. The point here simply reflects the fact that the high view of Christ's humanity comes finally to be associated with Alexandria after the christological debates of the fourth and fifth centuries.

43. Athanasius, *On the Incarnation* (Crestwood: St. Vladimir's Press, 1982), ch. 2, sect. 8.

44. An earlier version of the theses outlined in this section were published in "The Paschal Mystery and the 'Problem' of Human Suffering," *Sewanee Theological Review* 43:1 (Christmas 1999): 7–15.

45. Abelard's is sometimes cited as an exemplary theory of atonement but the adequacy of this claim is disputed; Clement of Alexandria's emphasis on the Word as teacher is also considered by some to be simply pedagogical and exemplary; yet, see Clement's language of regeneration in *Paedagogus*, Bk. I, ch. 6.

46. Anselm himself is clear in his image of God's love, not wrath, as the source of divine intervention in the human problem; yet, the feudal concern for the preservation of God's honor and his complex relation of compassion to justice sometimes make it difficult for his work to resist cooptation by such thin soteriologies. E.g.,

Anselm, *Why God Became Man,* trans. by S. N. Deane (LaSalle: Open Court Classics, 1962), Bk. I, chs. 12 and 24.

47. Solemn Collects of Good Friday according to the *Book of Common Prayer* 1979.

48. This is the key to the connection between the Triduum and the balance of the liturgical year. The Triduum crytallizes the Christian sensibilities that emerge from the diverse and multi-textured thematics of the liturgical year; the liturgical year fleshes out and elaborates the content of the Triduum.

49. Herman-Emiel Mertens, *Not the Cross But the Crucified,* 171.

50. Recall the linguistic roots of suffering in the permanently ambivalent nexus of the terms *passio* and *transitus*; suffering is closely related to the passage of time.

51. Revelation 5:6; 7:17.

52. *BCP,* 285.

53. Hebrews 4:15: "For we do not have a high priest who is unable to sympathize with our weaknesses, but we have one who in every respect has been tested as we are, yet without sin."

54. Ecclesiastes 9:11ff; Matthew 5:45; John 9:1–7. It is interesting to note that, in the first readings of the Great Vigil, the creation story is optional, but the Exodus story is not. The latter must always be read at the celebration. In the logic of the Triduum, God's love for those who suffer, cause notwithstanding, is the non-negotiable backdrop to the proclamation of the resurrection.

55. For a theological account, see Wendy Farley, *Tragic Vision and Divine Compassion* (Louisville: Westminster Press, 1990).

56. Taft, "What Does Liturgy Do?," 140–141. Taft's instincts are similar to Karl Barth's: "Thus [Jesus Christ] is in his person the covenant in its fulness, the close at hand Kingdom of Heaven, in which God speaks and humanity hears....God's glory shines in the highest—but also from the highest into the depths—and peace on earth eventuates among the people of his good pleasure. And just in this way, as this mediator and reconciler between God and humanity, Jesus Christ is for both *revealer*. Who and what God is in truth, and who and what humanity, we have not to explore and construct by roving freely far and near, but to read it where the truth about both dwells, in the fulness of their union, their covenant, their fulness which manifests itself in Jesus Christ." See "The Humanity of God," in *Karl Barth: Theologian of Freedom,* ed. by Clifford Green (Minneapolis: Fortress Press, 1991), 53.

57. The phrase is Han Frei's, and the liturgical theology developed herein is close

to the kind of theology he describes as "Type 4." See Hans Frei, *Types of Christian Theology* (New Haven: Yale University, 1992), 38–41.

58. Consider Eusebius's work that, contrary to the distance Augustine posited between the "two cities," presents the developments of Christian ascendancy as providential. The master narrative of Christian ascendancy involves an abstraction from the concrete suffering of human persons; the narrative of modernity gradually reverses the ascendancy of Christianity, but the abstraction from suffering endures.

59. Metz, *Faith in History and Society*, 132.

60. Ibid., 100ff.

CHAPTER SIX

Freeing the Formative Power of the Liturgy

THE RICH PRACTICAL RESOURCE of the Triduum for the formation of a people attentive to human suffering can be obscured by many things, not least of which are poor conditions of ritual performance. We conclude our inquiry, then, with a practical examination of some of the performative issues that can rob the Triduum of its formative power or twist its deep logic to another end.

The relationship between a rite and its performance is a complicated one. On the one hand, the structure of a rite has an integrity of its own from which emerges the contours of the theology enacted by the people who perform it. Carefully executed—that is, executed with full attention to the structure of the rite—the rite is freed for the full impact of its power to form sensibilities, inculcate moral commitments, school affections, and transform identity. On the other hand, the performance of the rite can, under the pressure of poor presiding, confused or untutored aims in execution, cultural or local resistance to its theology, or misappropriation of the rite for external purposes, lose its formative power. Those who apply hermeneutics and semiotics to liturgy are especially concerned with performance as a condition of liturgical meaning.[1] The analysis of the theology of a rite, too, includes certain judgments about its proper performance, and vice versa. The rite is, after all, *enacted* theology.

This circle of mutual interpretation is part and parcel of the relation between the *lex orandi* and the *lex credendi* embedded in ritual practice. The analysis of pastoral and practical considerations in the performance of the rite can be distinguished from the exposition of its theology but not separated from it. Gordon Lathrop, whose liturgical-theological methodology we have adapted in analyzing the structural juxtapositions of the Triduum liturgy, acknowledges this inescapable connection between the ideality of structure and the locality of concrete practice in his transition from the "secondary liturgical theology" derived from the *ordo*, or deep structure of the liturgical rites as they are "consciously organized" over time, to the "pastoral liturgical theology" in which the *ordo* is turned back upon the particular local assembly to critique, reform, and enrich its practice. He describes the kind of secondary liturgical theology we have attempted here as the attempt to "fashion a cup so that people today may drink from the water-spring that is the liturgy," but that pastoral liturgical theology is required "to clear out the spring itself so that the water flows more freely."[2] With regard to his own project, which focuses on baptism and eucharist as the place where word and sign are set alongside one another in the practice of the "eighth day" Christian sabbath, he describes the task of pastoral liturgical theology:

> To evaluate a specific liturgical assembly we may ask whether those juxtapositions are present as the central business of this gathering. Does this community meet on Sunday with a sense of lively counterpoint to the whole week? Are the scriptures read at the center of the meeting as if they were the book of life itself? By one text set next to another and by the whole broken open in preaching, is the synaxis made to speak of God's grace in Christ? Is the meal held? Is it seen to be the eating and drinking of the meaning of the scrip-

tures? Is this word and meal understood as taking place in a hungry city and a hungry world? Are the prayers both thanksgiving and lament? Is the bath seen as the way one enters this assembly? These are questions the *ordo* raises. They are not simply matters of taste. They are questions of Christian identity.[3]

If the questions Lathrop raises in *Holy Things* are questions of Christian identity, so surely are the matters we have raised here regarding the secondary liturgical theology arising from the central Christian liturgies of the year. The largest part of this book has been devoted to an exploration of the paschal identity of the people of God who, in liturgy, enter into a way of life that attends openly to suffering as the arena of God's saving action. In doing so, I have hoped to address the concerns of Lyotard and confirm the instincts of Metz on the basis of the Triduum's shape and structure, pointing toward a constructive soteriology that encourages and inculcates sensitivity to suffering in keeping with the *ordo* of the Triduum.

It is now necessary to turn to the practical and pastoral considerations in the performance of the Triduum, to identify the key issues of performance that work in a mutual interaction with the way the rite is structured that either maximize or obscure the meaning of the rite. The liturgy of the Triduum, given its still-recent recovery and due to a number of common errors in celebrating the rite, is surely a spring that bears clearing so that the waters of its dangerous memory of suffering may overflow the bounds of a culture bent on suppressing such memory to the detriment of those who suffer.

Broad Issues of Performance

If the wellspring of the Triduum liturgy is to flow freely, it must first flow. After some thirty years since the recovery of the Triduum in the Episcopal

Church USA, for example, many local congregations still do not observe
the Triduum at all. In too many places, the Easter liturgy of Holy
Eucharist is celebrated with vigorous planning and elaborate execution,
while Maundy Thursday is not celebrated at all and Good Friday, if celebrated, is reduced to an ecumenical service of meditation or other devotions that, aside from the singing of hymns, is relatively non-participatory.
The Vigil is still often ignored or, in a few cases, confused with the custom of the "sunrise service." Such practices are poor substitutes for the rich
soteriology of embodied servant love enacted in the Triduum liturgies. An
Easter liturgy celebrated by a congregation that has not felt the impact of
the intimate service of neighbor in the washing of feet, assumed the place
of Jesus Christ in praying for the world in all its pain and longing, or gazed
on the cross in holy defiance of the fear of facing suffering in all its power
is an Easter liturgy that will be little more than a cultural tradition of family gathering, a thinly disguised constantinian diversion, or a rite of spring.
The very logic of the Triduum demands the recognition that Easter does
not exist without Maundy Thursday and Good Friday. Anything less runs
the risk of underwriting in an unreflective way the modernist enchantment with pure positivity and the fear of suffering that perpetuates and
deepens the suffering of humanity.

Only a little less tragic than the practice of ignoring the Triduum altogether is the practice of observing the first two liturgies of the Triduum as
"special services" of Holy Week. Again, the problem here is the subtle separation of the power of risen life from the honest engagement with suffering humanity as the very mode of life and site through which God saves
us. Careful and consistent teaching and training of the congregation is necessary in order to avoid the sense that Maundy Thursday and Good Friday
liturgies are, however "special" or "moving" they may be, not central to the
Easter mystery. Care must be taken to teach how these rites are not mere
preliminary steps along the way to the celebration of new life, an idea that
works against the grain of the liturgies themselves. The paschal mystery is

celebrated in all three of the rites taken together: abundant life in self-giving service (Maundy Thursday); Christ's suffering as the supreme act of self-service that the church now embodies as its own mode of abundant life (Good Friday); incorporation into the community that is defined by the "dangerous memory" of that suffering as the source of new life by which we are continually nourished in the holy meal (Great Vigil of Easter). All three "moments" of the Triduum form the heart of the paschal mystery, and the celebration of the paschal mystery is the heart of a priestly people who find the way of the cross to be the way of life.

Clearing the Spring of the Triduum Liturgies

Even when the intrinsic connection among Maundy Thursday, Good Friday, and Easter is understood, there are pastoral-liturgical considerations in freeing the rites to exercise their full formative potential. The following major issues bear consideration because they are especially common errors and because they are, if not fatal to the structural intent of the rites, inconsistent with the Triduum *ordo*:

A. Replacing the Maundy Thursday rite with a Passover Seder;
B. Overly dramatizing the reservation of the sacrament on Maundy Thursday;
C. Depriving the people of the *mandatum*;
D. Replacing the Good Friday liturgy with meditations or stations of the cross;
E. Severely truncating the vigil readings in the Easter Vigil;
F. Celebrating the Easter Vigil without baptism;
G. In the Easter eucharist, failing to pray for those who suffer.

In addition to the foregoing, several other matters bear consideration in the planning and celebration of the Triduum:

H. The use of hymnody consistent with the inter-relationship of the liturgies;

I. Appropriate content, style, and length of preaching;

J. The decision on whether to include communion in the Good Friday liturgy;

K. The scheduling of the Vigil on Saturday night or Sunday morning;

L. The place of the people in the entrance procession;

M. The placement of baptism and the reading of the Easter gospel.

Because liturgy is not an abstraction, but a sequenced and formalized ordering of dense particulars of performance, the consideration of these issues is critical to "clearing the spring" of the Triduum liturgies.

Major Issues of Performance

A. Replacing the Maundy Thursday liturgy with a Passover Seder

It is a custom in some communities to celebrate a Passover Seder instead of the appointed liturgy for Maundy Thursday. It is easy to understand the intention in doing so as an acknowledgment of the theological roots of the Christian eucharist in the passover, and perhaps as a gesture of respect to the Jewish community from whose religious practice the Christian churches partly spring. The church is given an opportunity to experience firsthand the Jewish liturgical source of Christian eucharistic thematics. Maundy Thursday is taken to be the logical occasion for such an educational rite since, as we have seen, the establishment of the eucharist is the twin focus of the rite along with the *mandatum*.

While the intention is good, the effect of replacing the Maundy Thursday liturgy with a Seder runs contrary to the enacted theology of

the entire Triduum. In a Passover Seder, however meaningful and educational the experience may be, the very point of the exercise is the
problem: the historical distance between the normal eucharistic practice of the church and the passover meal in which the eucharist (at least
theologically if not also literally) was established shatters the anamnetic
quality of the Triduum. A living tradition for the Jewish people, the
Seder practiced in a Christian context has an inescapably educational
quality that hearkens back to the possible historical context of Jesus' last
supper with his disciples. In the Maundy Thursday liturgy, by contrast,
the relation between past and present is simultaneously preserved and
transgressed. The eucharist is celebrated as the meal in which Christ
the servant is given now in bread and wine to nourish us in our servant
way of life. This is the anamnetic power of Christ's presence called
forth in the singing of the Exsultet at the Vigil: "This is the night...."
in which Christ is present as *we* become Christ to the world, nourished
by his body and blood. This anamnetic memory, although bequeathed
to us by our Jewish forebears, does not mark the Christian experience
of the Jewish Passover Seder, which is a tradition external to the
Christian experience *of Christ* as the One by whom we "pass over" from
death to life.

For the Christian community, it is through the anamnetic power of
the practice of the *mandatum*, as well as the praying of the Solemn
Collects, the praise of God through the Exsultet, baptism, and the
eucharist, that Christ is present. The Seder can be a moving and educational experience, but an educational experience of a tradition not our
own, however important to our tradition, cannot take the place of the
formative quality of the Maundy Thursday liturgy in which the
Christian passover is not merely recalled in a historical sense, nor
mimetically enacted in drama, but entered into as the ritual transformation of ecclesial identity into Christ.

B. The Reservation of the Sacrament on Maundy Thursday

There is another common error made in the Maundy Thursday liturgy that works against its own deep structure. In most places, the altar and chancel are stripped at the end of the liturgy to heighten the solemnity of the events of Good Friday shortly to be the liturgical focus of the community, and to heighten the sense of Christ's presence *in absence* as we approach the observance of his physical death. Typically, a small portion of the consecrated bread and wine are reserved in a small chapel or other site. The primary purpose of this practice is to make it possible, where desired, to set aside consecrated elements for communion on Good Friday. All consecrated elements beyond what is needed for this practice are consumed or given reverently to the ground after the Maundy Thursday meal and the full liturgy of the eucharist is not celebrated on Good Friday.

Around this practice of reservation has arisen a devotional practice of the "watch" in which, throughout the night, someone is prayerfully present with the consecrated elements, as if to respond faithfully to Jesus' challenge to the disciples to "stay awake with me" in Gethsemane.[4]

In and of itself, the watch is not inconsistent with the refusal of the Christian community to shrink from the full force and reality of suffering that has been our concern in this paper, and that I have argued is the sensibility of the Triduum liturgies. Gazing upon the reserved sacrament and/or praying before the altar of repose after the *mandatum* and the incorporation of Christ's own body into our bodies in the eucharist is an experience not unlike the adoration of the cross on Good Friday that follows the Solemn Collects. In both cases, worshipers face with devotion the signs of Christ's suffering and death and of his absence from us that are, simultaneously, the signs of his life and presence to us. Also in both cases, ritual enactments of *ecclesia*-as-Christ are followed by acts that in some way restore the distance between Christ and the worshiper, preserving the complex dialectic between the church *as* Christ and the church *of* Christ, whose distinctive work is the ground and mystery into which we enter as life.[5] However, there is a caution that must be raised in regard to the watch service.

The church's enactment of its paschal identity in the Maundy Thursday liturgy is a corporate act: it is the whole gathered community, with all their gifts and limitations, that become Christ to the suffering world. The Triduum liturgies are weighted toward the formation of a *people*, and this social character of the paschal identity is central to the experience of salvation in which, ultimately, the whole world is drawn into the power of God's transforming presence. The devotions of the watch service are private, not corporate. While they encourage the clear-eyed recognition of suffering as do the Triduum liturgies as whole, they do not share their social-formational function that goes to the heart of salvation in Christ: we are saved by entering into Christ's abundant life of self-offering to the other *as a people*, or not at all.

In addition to the contrast between the private focus of the watch and the corporate focus of the Maundy Thursday liturgy, there is always a danger that the reservation of the sacrament as a site of personal devotion will displace the main purpose of communion that is to incorporate (literally) the body and blood of Christ into our own bodies by which we are incorporated into him. This mutual incorporation is at the center of the communion's role in the creation of a paschal people. It relies on the consumption of the consecrated bread and wine, which is the point of their consecration. This is also, again, the point of the reservation of the sacrament on Maundy Thursday: to provide the possibility for the ministration of the sacrament to the people of God on Good Friday.

The importance of consumption as the point of the eucharistic celebration can be made in terms of Augustine's scheme of relations between the eternal, historical, and mystical body of Christ, to which we gave attention in Chapter Four. The reader will recall that the sacramental power of the eucharist is situated, for Augustine, between its material

signification of the crucifixion and resurrection of Jesus Christ, in whom
the character of the eternal God is revealed, and, on the other hand, the
signification of ecclesial identity. The church receives the body and blood
of Christ in the eucharist, but that receipt is performative of the church's
own identity as the body and blood of Christ given to the world. To
reduce the eucharist to a sacramental presentation of Christ in the bread
and wine without its presentation of the mystical body of Christ in which
the church participates would simultaneously idolize the eucharist and
disconnect the church's liturgical action from its ethics. [6]

Both Roman Catholics (for whom the adoration of the sacrament
apart from its corporate consumption was long a feature of the personal
devotions of some of its members) and Anglicans are now in clear agree-
ment on the primary purpose of the sacrament as consumption.[7] While
both traditions allow for the adoration of the sacrament, both recognize
and work to minimize the risks involved in this practice. Educationally,
the church ought to ensure that the primary focus on Maundy Thursday
remains the *mandatum* and the communion of the people. Practically, in
parish and public communication, the "watch" before the reserved sacrament ought to be carefully considered so it does not overwhelm the
liturgy itself. Liturgically, where the sacrament is reserved after the
Maundy Thursday liturgy, the consecrated elements ought to be moved
to the altar of repose simply, without fanfare or long and elaborate pro-
cessionals with thuribles and banners, and the altar of repose itself should
be simple and understated. These measures will help to keep the adoration or "watch" before the sacrament from blocking the clear stream of
enacted theology of the Maundy Thursday liturgy.

C. Depriving the people of the mandatum

The *Book of Occasional Services* implies that the only form for the washing of feet on Maundy Thursday is for the priest to wash the feet of

members of the congregation. This symbol is not wrong-headed; despite the servant role of the priest in the congregation, priests also *preside* over the congregation's life, with the oversight of the bishop. Thus, it is an especially powerful symbol for the presider to wash the feet of congregation's members. The practice of the bishop or priest kneeling to wash the feet of the candidates for baptism—the newest members of the community—is highly commendable. However, there is no reason to restrict this act to the ordained presider. The symbol of the *mandatum* is only increased in its power by opening the act to the whole congregation. This can be arranged in any number of ways and is far superior to a third alternative, the washing of the feet of "representative" members of the congregation, which usually either establishes or reflects a hierarchy running counter to the very humility and service that the rite aims to enact.

D. Ritual Substitutes for the Good Friday Liturgy

Two ritual alternatives are sometimes substituted for the proper liturgy for Good Friday: Stations of the Cross and the three-hour "watch" service. The former is normally done in procession, with short readings, antiphons, and prayers at each of the "stations" or points of progression along the way from Jesus' trial to his crucifixion. Stations is a corporate practice that places the participants in a position as onlookers who desire to enter into the way of Jesus' suffering and death as they dramatically reenact his final steps. The procession normally begins at the altar, proceeds around the church or outside the church, perhaps in a garden or around the apse, and returns to the altar for a concluding prayer.

The three-hour "watch" service is a more recent innovation than Stations and is often ecumenical in character. Normally occurring from noon to three during the hours Jesus was thought to have hung on the cross, this service differs widely from place to place but involves a sequence of readings or meditations, homiletic offerings of meditations by local clergy, and musical anthems or hymns. The watch service is usually open for people to come and go as they can, although some stay for the entire three hours.

The limitations of replacing the Good Friday liturgy with the Stations or the watch service are clearly evident. Neither is in keeping with the spirit of the Good Friday liturgy. The latter, though public, is not typically high on the scale of corporate participation, which gives it the same limitations as the adoration of the reserved sacrament on Maundy Thursday night. Related to this and of high importance, the watch service does nothing to manuever or position the congregation in the place of Christ, which is the critical soteriological import of the Good Friday liturgy in its traditional form. The Stations come a bit closer to this intention, by walking the people through the way of the cross with their own bodies. Still, there is no particular ritual attention given to the full assumption of the paschal identity by the people; they remain, primarily, onlookers, albeit active ones, and the service never closes the gap between the identity of those who pray for the grace of a cruciform life and their ritual assumption of that life as one poured out in self-offering to the world.

The watch service, of little value aside from its encouragement of ecumenical prayer, should be let go as a Good Friday observance. Stations of the Cross, if they are held at all, are an appropriate devotional practice if held at a time other than the traditional hour of the Good Friday liturgy (twelve noon).

E. The Vigil Readings at Easter

We have seen how the delight of new life at Easter is not a final or triumphalist conclusion of pain and suffering, but continues to remember and honor suffering and death, however painful, as the continuing site of God's saving presence. At the same time, the pain and suffering anticipated on Maundy Thursday and recalled on Good Friday involves, already, the bodily knowledge of the resurrection to new life in and through that suffering. Where the inter-relationship between these liturgies is minimized by inadequate performance or even the failure to perform the Triduum at all, Easter becomes a triumph over death without remainder and, at that very point, ceases to be an authentic Christian celebration of life. Even where the first two liturgies of the Triduum are properly celebrated, the Vigil can lose its soteriological power if it is altered in certain ways. One common alteration that cripples the Vigil's power to honor the open and continuing character of human suffering is the shortening of the Vigil readings.

The Vigil readings take place just after the lighting and procession of the New Fire and the singing of the Exsultet. Thus placed, they heighten the tension between the anamnetic presence of Christ, symbolized and lauded in the paschal candle that has been placed in the sight of all, and the absence of Christ, felt as the raw pain of the condition of human suffering and ritualized in the longing for Christ expressed in the cardinal scriptures of the Old Testament. Rereading these passages, and responding in antiphon and song, the congregation appropriates the longing for redemption expressed in the vigil readings right in the midst of their celebration of Christ's presence.

To express longing adequately *takes time*; phenomenologically, longing and promise are tied to a sense of time in the experience of "not-yet," of waiting. This experience of taking time, of acknowledging the "not-yet" of salvation right in the midst of the liturgy that celebrates salvation, is what gives the Easter celebration the character of a "vigil" in the first place. For practical reasons, the congregational experience of taking time—of acknowledging that the salvation entered into is, at the same time, a salvation still awaited—is often truncated because, quite simply, the presiding clergy are concerned about the service becoming "too long."

This common concern raises questions about our impatience and inability to sustain ambiguity and a lack of closure that are characteristics

not unrelated to the modern predilection for rapid progress toward closure and the suppression of suffering. This concern also raises questions
about our willingness, as a community, to allow the time of the liturgy to
shape our own sense of time, however uncomfortable or inconvenient
that may be, or whether the practice of liturgy must conform to our con-
venience. By contrast, in God's time we learn to tarry and wait and discover God's presence at the very place where things are incomplete,
people suffer, and the world longs for redemption. The Great Vigil of
Easter inculcates such a sense of God's time by the rhythmic repetition
of hearing and response that occurs in the vigil readings.

Nine readings are included in the 1979 *Book of Common Prayer*; the
rubrics require that at least two be read, one of which must be the account
of the conclusion of the Passover with Israel's deliverance at the Red
Sea.[8] This is an ill-advised minimum. At least four or five readings
should be included, if not all nine. Any tedium that might set in during
the full complement of readings can be ameliorated by the dramatic
treatment of at least some of them—for example, the use of two lectors
for the reading from the dialogue between Ezekiel and God—which at
any rate brings the readings to life. Thus lingering over the readings, the
people maintain both sides of the Triduum's dialectic: they celebrate salvation amidst the ritualized rehearsal of longing and the awareness of the
suffering that continues.

F. Baptism at the Easter Eucharist

Of all times during the Christian year, Easter is the most appropriate
for baptism. This is due to the fact that the Triduum liturgies are the
liturgies most concerned with the formation of Christian paschal identity—the formation of a people as Christ for the world—and baptism
is the primary ritual of initiation into Christ. To celebrate the Great
Vigil of Easter without celebrating baptism is to miss the opportunity

to initiate new members into Christ's life at the point where the nature of Christ's life is most clearly in evidence. Some churches decline to baptize at Easter for the same reason that they severely truncate the vigil readings: they are concerned that the liturgy will "take too long." Once again, in this case, the impatience for closure and the insistence that liturgy must conform to our temporal expectations rather than shape them, undermines the deep interest of the Triduum liturgies in identity formation, with which baptism is also primarily concerned. At the least, if there are no baptisms on Easter, the reaffirmation of baptismal vows should take their place, although this is a fairly anemic substitute for actual baptisms.

The Easter Vigil is an especially appropriate time for the baptism of adults, following on a catechumenal process that centers on preparation for the assumption of the paschal identity. The preparation of adult catechumens for baptism at Easter, who freely choose to leave their old identity and assume a new one in Christ, heightens for them and for the congregation the church's discontinuity with the culture of modernity.

G. Missing the opportunity to pray for those who suffer

Although the Triduum, observed with due attention to the practical issues of performance we have discussed, lifts up the reality of suffering in the midst of life and attends to the power of life in the midst of suffering, there is one opportunity to further heighten the awareness of suffering in the Easter liturgy in a way consistent with the deepest instincts of the Triduum. This opportunity hinges on the selection of the eucharistic prayer for use on Maundy Thursday and especially at the Easter Vigil.

The 1979 *Book of Common Prayer* contains an ecumenical eucharistic prayer adapted from the Egyptian anaphora of St. Basil, known in that book as "Prayer D."[9] This prayer is especially appropriate for use at the

Great Vigil of Easter because it is used by several Christian traditions that, despite their many differences, share in the fundamental character of the paschal identity. Additionally, it is the most sweeping in scope of the eucharistic prayers, consistent with the sweeping scope of salvation history and prophecy in the vigil readings. While its use involves the loss of the variable preface for Easter that is inserted in other eucharistic prayers, this is not really a significant loss. The already strong paschal imagery of Prayer D's fixed preface, post-sanctus, and supplication is sufficient for Triduum usage.

Beyond being commended by theological aesthetics and ecumenical concerns, Prayer D reflects the West Syrian structure, allowing the presider to include local concerns and intercessions in the body of the prayer itself. The use of this eucharistic prayer thus provides a prime opportunity to name and acknowledge the people and nations of the world whose very current experience of life is one marked by suffering. Nothing could be more consistent with the whole tenor of the Triduum than to include in the victorious prayer, at whose heart Jesus' own suffering is recalled, the names or conditions of those who suffer at the very moment at which the Easter liturgy is celebrated. The choice of other eucharistic prayers, while not incorrect, misses an opportunity for the intent of the Solemn Collects of Good Friday to be extended into the eucharistic prayer itself.

Other Considerations in the Celebration of the Triduum Liturgies

The foregoing considerations are key issues in a pastoral liturgical theology attentive to the *ordo* of the Triduum liturgies. There are several other considerations of some import, however, to which we must turn briefly before concluding our assessment of performative issues.

H. Hymnody in the Triduum

The shape of the liturgies and their formative power are as much aesthetic as theological; indeed, the false separation of the aesthetic from
the rational that characterizes modernity is put to the lie in ritual practice, where the rational "content" or meaning of liturgy is of a piece with
the shape, structure, and tone of the rites as they shape the identity of
the practitioners. The poetics of hymnody are partly shaped by the
rubrics that place anthems and hymns within the overall structure of the
liturgy, but the presider must take care to choose hymnic content consistent with the theology enacted in and through that structure. Hymns
and anthems should reflect the deep and complex inter-relationship
between suffering and salvation, between life and death that the
Triduum celebrates. Dolorous hymns that ponder Christ's suffering or
especially sentimental hymns should be avoided on Maundy Thursday
and Good Friday, as should hymns that reflect a triumphalist experience
of resurrection and the complete conquest of death without remainder
on Easter.[10]

One additional problem can occur with the Good Friday liturgy: of
all the Triduum rites, this liturgy generates its rhetorical and aesthetic
power by its relative compactness, especially as it moves very quickly
from the adoration of the cross to the closing prayer and silent departure of the people; yet, this one service of the year seems, in many
places, to be so overburdened with long hymns and anthems that it
loses its sense of movement. This is not a question of the time-worn
battle among liturgists on whether the music serves the word, or vice-
versa; it is a question of how both music and word, together, are pro-
portionately balanced so as to express, and not obscure, the underlying
structure of the rite.

I. Content, style, and length of preaching

This brings us to the word proclaimed in the homily, in which concerns
with theological aesthetics must also be applied. The shape and contours
of the Triduum, with its symmetrical paschal relation of suffering and
life, should be reflected in miniature in the content of preaching. Easter
sermons that fail to incarnate the paradox of the power of new life arising in and through suffering and death are little more than religious
expressions of hope in the modern myth. Conversely, preaching on
Maundy Thursday and Good Friday should focus on this same paradox
from the other side: new life is found in the suffering service of the other
whose own suffering is not to be feared. For all the terror of the crucifixion, the preacher does well to sketch a vision of it not simply as the effect
of sin, even less as the punishment for it, but as the length to which Jesus'
loving, life-giving service of the world would take him.

     The length of the homily in the Triduum liturgies is equally important.
Preachers who *do* understand the significance of these liturgies are sometimes inclined to overreach in the length and tone of their sermons. In
fact, the Triduum liturgies are powerful enough that they almost "preach
themselves," and sermons that are overly long or serious can sometimes
shift the weight of the rite away from, for example, the *mandatum* or the
Solemn Collects, where the emphasis properly belongs. The preacher
should take care to illustrate the meaning of these elements of the
Triduum rites, not supplant their place by sermons that try to summarize
the whole of Christian faith on a single homiletic occasion.

J. Collects, Cross, and Communion at the Good Friday liturgy

Three aspects of the Good Friday liturgy invite special attention by
presiders and planners. First, the rubrics allow the Solemn Collects to be
adapted as appropriate to the local congregation. As the daily news

brings fresh, hourly word of human travail around the planet, planners do well keep the church's prayers fresh and attentive to current needs. The repetition of familiar language is important to ritual formation but can also stultify and lull a congregation into half-hearing their own prayers. Not only in the Solemn Collects of Good Friday, but every Sunday, the intercessions should be current and accessible so that the people can truly *pray* for the plight of those who suffer.

It is recommended that the whole congregation be involved in the Solemn Collects as well. Prayer book rubrics reflect a preference that the deacon offer the opening bidding of the prayers, and the deacon may offer each set of the prayers with the concluding collect offered by the celebrant. A better practice is to reserve the opening bidding to the deacon, following with the offering of the prayers by various members of the congregation, with the celebrant concluding each as specified. This practice involves several orders of ministry in a critical work that ultimately belongs to them all and brings home the participation of the whole congregation in the intercessory dimension of Christ's priestly ministry in which they share.

Second, for the veneration of the cross, the prayer book rubrics specify the use of "a wooden cross" but offer no additional direction about its proportions or character. Of course, the cross ought to be of a size suitable to its symbolic significance. Some congregations utilize a *crucifix* for the purpose of veneration. The question is whether a crucifix, with the corpus of the crucified Jesus affixed on it, or a plain, empty cross is a more apt focus of piety for this day in which the congregation simultaneously lingers over the suffering of God in Christ and honors the cross as a symbol of new life. The choice to use a crucifix is not catastrophic, but the forthrightness of a plain wooden cross may be more compelling in its simplicity and a more productive focus for the symbolic imagination.

By long tradition, Eucharist is not celebrated on Good Friday, but that tradition is neither historically nor regionally universal. In certain times and places, at least, communion from the reserved sacrament has been brought from the altar of repose for the communion of the people. Those who argue for this practice often argue simply that of all days, the people should receive communion on Good Friday. This argument reflects, perhaps, an inclination to see each of the Triduum liturgies as separate rites standing alone, and fails to appreciate the way in which Eucharist is already a part of the experience of the Christian pasch by its practice on Maundy Thursday and Easter. There is probably little harm done to the enacted theology of the Triduum by having communion on this day, since communion shares with the Solemn Collects the effect of incorporating or "fusing" the identity of the people with that of Christ. On the other hand, communion may shortchange the aesthetic power of the Good Friday liturgy, which is partly a function of its coming to a quick end with a brief prayer and departure in silence, just after the adoration of the cross. Communion is presented in the Episcopal *Book of Common Prayer* as an option not specifically part of the Good Friday liturgy, and is perhaps best left undone except where the piety of the congregation is so eucharistically-centered as to render them unable to celebrate Good Friday without it.

K. The scheduling of the Great Vigil of Easter

Given the liturgical rhythm of Christian festivals that reflects the Jewish commitment to the advent of the new day at sundown, the Great Vigil of Easter can be celebrated at any time between sundown on Saturday and sunrise on Sunday morning. Eastern Orthodox churches, even in North America, keep to the ancient practice of beginning late Saturday evening and continuing through the night into Sunday morning; western churches, whose Vigil is shorter, tend to opt for one or the other. From one point of view, there is little difference between the two options, leaving the presider to balance the powerful effect of the lighting of the

New Fire in the pitch black of night against the pre-dawn gray-black sky, or to weigh the scheduling of the Vigil in relation to what are often multiple Easter eucharists that follow it later in the morning. Before making this decision based on these local pragmatic factors, it is worth pondering the nature of the Vigil *as a vigil*—specifically, as a celebration of salvation in the midst of continued longing and suffering.

Some argue that the celebration of the Vigil on Easter morning, beginning in the pre-dawn darkness and ending in the bright light of the sun, works against that quality of vigil, so close to the heart of the enacted theology of the Triduum, as we have seen. The elemental human experience of the sunrise, giving birth to metaphors such as "the dawn of a new day," may actually work against the Easter Vigil's intent to celebrate resurrection by remembering the death through which it emerges and that continues to haunt the human experience. Conversely, the celebration of the Vigil on Easter eve in which, following the dismissal, the people spill out of the church into a world cloaked in night, may support and underline the quality of the service *as vigil*.[11] Whatever local clergy decide in the scheduling of this rite, they are well reminded that the context and time of a liturgy's celebration become part of the liturgy itself, and must be taken with utmost seriousness in the process of planning.

L. The Place of the People in the Entrance Procession

Presiders and liturgical planners express among themselves divergent opinions on whether the procession of the New Fire into the sacred space should be the head of a procession of all the people, or whether the procession of the New Fire should enter a darkened church where the people, already gathered, await its entry. Local concerns have much to do with this decision, as the Episcopal prayer book makes clear that the opening exhortation given at the lighting is to be addressed to the people, implying that they be in proximity to the fire or able to see and hear the place where it is lit.

The decision of whether to lead the people in by the Paschal candle or bring it into them where they wait in darkness points up an interesting tension in the theology of the liturgy, to which we have already alluded. In the etymological foundation of the paschal terminology, it is permanently undecidable whether the focus of the celebration is on *passio* (suffering, passion, pathos) or *transitus* (passage, movement, pilgrimage). It may be argued that the two alternatives to the procession of the Fire evoke, in the aesthetics of the liturgy, each of these in turn. Placing the people in the procession behind the Fire involves a sense of passage, as the people move, like those of the Exodus, on a journey from the darkness to the sacred space, illuminated by a light not unlike that of the pillar of fire by which God led the Hebrews in their journey from bondage to freedom. To the contrary, the gathering of the people in near-total darkness in the church evokes the longing, desolation, and blindness of those who cannot see beyond their suffering until they are illuminated, suddenly, by the merciful glow of the paschal fire. In the end, this particular decision seems appropriately decided by pragmatic concerns of the local context of celebration. Either alternative seems consistent with the deep structure of the rite.

M. The order of baptism and the reading of the Easter gospel

More commonly than not, baptism is celebrated at the end of the Vigil readings and prior to the proclamation of the Easter gospel. More specifically the order proceeds as follows:

- Lighting of the New Fire and Procession
- Singing of the Exsultet
- Vigil Readings (Old Testament)

- Baptisms
- Easter liturgy of the Word: Epistle and Resurrection Gospel
- Sermon
- (Prayers)
- Peace

This is a dramatic alternative, as baptism done by candlelight (the only light burning at this point in the liturgy) is quite beautiful, and is probably the factor that commends this order in many places. It is allowed by the rubrics of the Episcopal prayer book. Nevertheless, there is a problem with this order that one must consider.

There is, in the Triduum liturgies, no less than in the regular Sunday celebration of the eucharist, a deep structure of hearing and response embedded in the prescribed order of elements. On a normal Sunday, for example, the proclamation of both the promissory voice of the Old Testament and the gospel announcement of the work of Christ sets the context of understanding for those called to baptism. Having heard the gospel proclaimed and sermonized in its fullness, the baptized then enter the life to which that gospel calls them by water and oil, then by bread and wine. First, the Word, then the response of discipleship and communion in the mystery of the proclaimed Lord. This is the deep sensibility of Christian devotional life, and the pattern of grace from one who "first loved us."[12]

In the Triduum liturgies, the gospel proclamation is even more important to this pattern of hearing and response than on a normal Sunday. It is not simply by virtue of some innate attractiveness to the servant life, but by the valoritzation of that servanthood as the way of Life—a valorization that occurs through the announcement of the resurrection gospel—that the candidates for baptism are drawn into the eucharistic community. Placing the baptism before that announcement interrupts the normal pattern of hearing and response. It appears to separate the passion and suffering of Christ, and the promise of new Life, from the instantiation of that new Life through the resurrection. The following order would be more consistent with that deep structure and would do better to bind the paradox of suffering and salvation, death and life, sorrow and hope together as the matrix of the baptismal formation into which the candidates enter.

- Lighting of the New Fire and Procession
- Singing of the Exsultet
- Vigil Readings (Old Testament)
- Easter liturgy of the Word: Epistle and Resurrection Gospel
- Baptisms
- Sermon
- Peace

Though this eliminates the intercessions other than those offered for the baptismal candidates, additional intercessions could be included in eucharistic Prayer D.

Concluding Observations

It is my hope that the details of liturgical performance to which we have given consideration will help not only in the planning of these liturgies by priests, musicians, and liturgists, but that, more importantly, they serve to illuminate the enacted theology of those liturgies as such. Such is the purpose of a pastoral liturgical theology in clearing the stream of liturgy, so that the living waters of the Christ who suffers in us and saves us can more fully empower us in worship. In the last analysis, that worship leads to joy as we approach the font and the altar inspired to remember the world to God, only to discover that Christ already remembers us before God in all our distractions, confusion, and pain, and saves us precisely there. To this humbling discovery, the only possible response is to redouble our willingness to be shaped and formed into a paschal people, to love the world as Christ loves us, and to give thanks.

Notes

1. Hughes, *Worship as Meaning;* Joyce Ann Zimmerman, *Liturgy and Hermeneutics* (Collegeville: Liturgical Press, 1999).

2. Lathrop, *Holy Things,* 7.

3. Ibid., 162.

4. Matthew 26:39–41; Mark 14:36–38.

5. See the discussion of exemplarity and solidarity, p. 108 above.

6. Again, see Augustine's Tractate 26, in *Tractates on the Gospel of John,* 271. Cf. Aquinas: "What this sacrament signifies and causes is the unity of Christ's mystical body, the church, the one ark in the flood outside of which there is no salvation....Notice that bodily food nourishes by being changed into the eater's own substance, and what is needed to preserve our life is its physical consumption. But our spiritual food changes us into itself: *you will not change me into yourself as you do the food of your flesh, but you will be changed into me.*...the eucharist is a sign of Christ's suffering bringing men into finished unity with the Christ who suffered." See Thomas Aquinas, *Summa Theologiae: A Concise Translation,* ed. by Timothy McDermott (Westminster: Christian Classics 1989), 569.

7. Anglican-Roman Catholic International Commission, *The Final Report* (London: SPCK, 1982), 23–24. For the historic position of the Episcopal Church on this issue, see Article XXVIII in *BCP,* 873.

8. *BCP,* 288.

9. *BCP,* 372. See Jasper and Cuming, *Prayers of the Eucharist,* 67ff.

10. One Episcopal priest known to this author insists each year on replacing the *Pange lingua* ("Sing my tongue, the glorious battle"), a hymn richly expressive of the priestly character of Christ in the crucifixion, with "The Old Rugged Cross," a sentimental favorite of considerably thinner musical and theological value.

11. The celebration of the Vigil on Saturday night is recommended by Louanne Bachner for this reason; the present author shares her considered opinion.

12. See Bachner, "Fire, Story, Water, Feast," 96ff.

EPILOGUE

IN THE PROCESS of discussing the epistolary communicative patterns of the early Christian communities, Rowan Williams characterizes the early church's discourse as "an interwoven plurality of perspectives on what was transacted in Jerusalem."[1] This is an apt description of the soteriological plurality of Christian theology. Christological doctrine has been debated and regularized through conciliar agreements, but soteriology has never been subject to the same kind of regularization. This, I suggest, is rooted in an ecclesial intuition that the enormous mystery at the heart of Christianity—the "savingness" of Christ for us—is of such significance for the totality of human experience that no single theory or doctrinal definition is adequate to its breadth or depth. Soteriological plurality is, for this reason, even more important to guard than the ontological and metaphysical speculations of christological orthodoxy.

The soteriology I have presented in these pages is not an exception to this rule of Christian discourse. There are other soteriological possibilites than the one I have presented, even within the 1979 *Book of Common Prayer*. If one were to analyze each and every prayer, collect, bidding, anaphora, and antiphon of the prayer book, one would find many different soteriological images and ideas. What I have attempted to do here is to render the soteriology that emerges at the structural level when many of those prayers are configured in a certain way within a particular set of rites and in relation to other rites of the prayer book. Thus configured, certain images and ideas drop into the background, others come into the foreground. In the Holy Week liturgies, the core liturgies of the year, suffering comes into the foreground and is caught up in the death and resurrection of Christ, the great mystery into which Christians enter by baptism and by which they are nourished in the eucharist. This soteriology brings an important voice to the ongoing discourse of Christian theology.

The paschal soteriology we have explored herein is not meant to ascribe error or inadequacy to other soteriological possibilities of historical Christianity in any absolute sense. Theories of propitiation, moral exemplarity, satisfaction, existential healing, *theosis*, or the conquest of death each have had something to offer to Christian reflection *within the context from which each emerged*. What I do suggest is that the paschal soteriology presented here may have the advantage over other models in our *present* context. That context is marked by two dominant concerns for theology: (1) our awareness of the enormity of suffering attached to the human condition; and (2) our concern for the inherent power of abstraction in theoretical thinking to erase, reinscribe, or explain human suffering in a way that actually increases its amount and intensity for humanity.

We have attempted to show, in these pages, that these concerns do not form a new problematic to which Christian theology must adapt. Christian faith, and the theology that elaborates its lived character, always and already speaks to these concerns because God has spoken to these concerns through Christ's priestly work, drawing our suffering into the divine life and offering salvation at the very point of our suffering.

Coupled with these two contemporary concerns in theology is our awareness that it is neither impossible to escape theoretical argument in theology, nor desirable to do so. Instead, we seek to speak theoretically and systematically in a way that is self-aware with regard to these concerns. We seek to think, speak, and argue theologically as an activity of *witness* to the suffering of human persons, so that theology, though necessarily an activity of theoretical human reasoning, remains faithful to the God of Jesus Christ, who cares for those who suffer.[2]

It is tempting to imagine that not only the desire to repress suffering but the enormity of human suffering is a monster *created* by the modern age. I trust it is clear from these pages that I do not believe this to be so—only that the conceptual categories of the modern climate make it difficult to address human travail with dignity and honesty, and that the Christian faith nurtured in Holy Week may help Christians to act differently. But it has always been the night. Annie Dillard once wrote:

> There were no formerly heroic times, and there was no formerly pure generation. There is no one here but us chickens, and so it has always been: a people busy and powerful, knowledgeable, ambivalent, important, fearful, and self-aware; a people who scheme, promote, deceive and conquer; who pray for their loved ones, and long to flee misery and skip death. It is a weakening and discoloring idea, that rustic people knew God once upon a time—or even knew selflessness or courage or literature—but that it is too late for us. In fact, the absolute is available to everyone in every age. There never was a more holy age than ours, and never a less. There is no less holiness at this time—as you are reading this—than there was the day the Red Sea parted, or that day, in the thirtieth year, in the fourth month, on the fifth day of the month, as Ezekiel was a captive by the river Chebar, when the heavens opened and he saw visions of God.[3]

There is comfort in knowing that it has always been night, if one also knows the consolation of a genuine hope in the power of God to bring life from death. May Christians everywhere find the capacity to suffer with hope during this long night, the compassion to carry the burden of others, and the joy of anticipation that God will ever make our suffering the arena of the divine power to save.

May they finally be able, with all the people of the world, to pray to God with the psalmist:

If I climb up to heaven, you are there;
if I make the grave my bed, you are there also.
If I take the wings of the morning
and dwell in the uttermost parts of the sea,
Even there your hand will lead me
and your right hand hold me fast.
If I say, "Surely the darkness will cover me,
and the light around me turn to night,"
Darkness is not dark to you;
the night is as bright as the day;
darkness and light to you are both alike. (Psalm 139:8–12)

Notes

1. Rowan Williams, "Does It Make Sense to Speak of a Pre-Nicene Orthodoxy?" in *The Making of Orthodoxy: Essays in Honour of Henry Chadwick*, ed. by Rowan Williams (Cambridge: Cambridge University, 1989), 2.

2. See Rebecca Chopp, "Theology and the Poetics of Testimony," unpublished paper, Emory University, n.d.

3. Annie Dillard, *For the Time Being* (New York: Alfred A. Knopf, 1999), 88–89.

WORKS CITED

Alison, James. *The Joy of Being Wrong: Original Sin through Easter Eyes*. New York: Crossroad Publishing, 1998.

Ambrose. *On the Sacraments and On the Mysteries*. J. H. Strawley, ed. T. Thompson, trans. London: SPCK, 1950.

Anderson, E. Byron, and Bruce T. Morrill, eds. *Liturgy and the Moral Self: Humanity at Full Stretch Before God*. Collegeville: Liturgical Press, 1998.

Anglican-Roman Catholic Commission. *The Final Report*. London: SPCK, 1982.

Anselm. *Why God Became Man*. S. N. Deane, trans. LaSalle: Open Court Classics, 1962.

Aquinas, Thomas. *Summa Theologiae: A Concise Translation*. Timothy McDermott, ed. Westminster: Christian Classics, 1989.

Ashley, James Matthew. *Interruptions: Mysticism, Politics, and Theology in the Work of Johann Baptist Metz*. Notre Dame: University of Notre Dame, 1998.

Athanasius. *On the Incarnation*. Crestwood: St. Vladimir's Press, 1982.

Augustine. *Sermons III/10*. In *The Works of Saint Augustine: A Translation for the 21st Century.* Edmund Hill, O.P., trans. Hyde Park: New City Press, 1990.

———. "Tractates on the Gospel of John, 11–27." In *The Fathers of the Church.* John W. Rettig, trans. Washington, D.C.: Catholic University of America Press, 1988.

Bachner, Louanne Kathryn. "Fire, Story, Water, Feast: An Exploration of Liturgical Theology and the Poetics of Celebration in the Easter Vigil Liturgy." Ph.D. dissertation, Emory University, 1990.

Barth, Karl. *Church Dogmatics* 3/2. G. W. Bromiley and T. F. Torrance, eds. Edinburgh: T & T Clark, 1960.

———. "The Humanity of God." In *Karl Barth: Theologian of Freedom.* Clifford Green, ed. Minneapolis: Fortress Press, 1991.

Bartlett, Anthony W. *Cross Purposes: The Violent Grammar of Christian Atonement.* Harrisburg: Trinity Press International, 2001.

The Bible. New Revised Standard Version. Bruce M. Metzger and Roland E. Murphy, eds. New York: Oxford University Press, 1991.

The Book of Common Prayer. New York: Seabury Press, 1979.

The Book of Occasional Services. New York: Church Hymnal, 1994.

Bradshaw, Paul F. " '*Diem baptismo sollemniorum*': Initiation and Easter in Christian Antiquity." In *Living Water, Sealing Spirit.* Maxwell E. Johnson, ed. Collegeville: Liturgical Press, 1995.

———. *The Search for the Origins of Christian Worship.* 2nd ed. Oxford: Oxford University Press, 2002.

Brawley, Robert L. "*Anamnesis* and Absence in the Lord's Supper." In *Biblical Theology Bulletin* (Winter 1990): 139–146.

Brock, Rita Nakashima, and Rebecca Ann Parker. *Proverbs of Ashes: Violence, Redemptive Suffering, and the Search for What Saves Us.* Boston: Beacon Press, 2001.

Cavanaugh, William T. *Torture and Eucharist: Theology, Politics, and the Body of Christ.* Oxford: Blackwell Publishers, 1998.

Chauvet, Louis-Marie. *Symbol and Sacrament.* Patrick Madigan, S.J., and Madeleine Beaumont, trans. Collegeville: Liturgical Press, 1995.

Chopp, Rebecca. *The Praxis of Suffering: An Interpretation of Liberation and Political Theologies.* Maryknoll: Orbis Books, 1986.

————. "Theology and the Poetics of Testimony." Unpublished paper, Emory University, n.d.

Clement of Alexandria. *Christ the Educator [Paedagogus].* New York: Fathers of the Church, Inc., 1954.

Collins, Mary. *Worship: Renewal to Practice.* Washington, D.C.: Pastoral Press, 1987.

Colombo, J. A. *An Essay on Theology and History: Studies in Pannenberg, Metz, and the Frankfurt School.* Atlanta: Scholar's Press, 1990.

Connerton, Paul. *How Societies Remember.* Cambridge: Cambridge University Press, 1989.

Cranmer, Thomas. *Miscellaneous Writings and Letters of Thomas Cranmer.* John Edmund Cox, ed. Cambridge: Cambridge University Press, 1846.

Crichton, J. D. *The Liturgy of Holy Week.* Dublin: Veritas Press, 1983.

DeConcini, Barbara. *Narrative Remembering.* Lanham: University Press of America, 1990.

The Didache. In *Early Christian Fathers.* Cyril C. Richardson, trans. and ed. New York: MacMillan Publishing Company, 1970.

Didascalia Apostolorum. R. Hugh Connolly, trans. Oxford: Clarendon Books, 1929.

Dillard, Annie. *For the Time Being.* New York: Alfred A. Knopf, 1999.

Egeria's Travels. John Wilkinson, trans. and ed. London: SPCK, 1971.

Eigo, Francis. "The Easter Vigil: An Historical, Theological, and Pastoral Study." Ph.D. dissertation, Catholic University of America, 1969.

Enriching Our Worship. New York: Church Pension Fund, 1998.

Fagerberg, David. *What Is Liturgical Theology?* Collegeville: Liturgical Press, 1992.

Farley, Wendy. *Tragic Vision and Divine Compassion.* Louisville: Westminster Press, 1990.

Frei, Hans. *Types of Christian Theology.* George Hunsinger and William C. Placher, eds. New Haven: Yale University Press, 1992.

Gaillard, Jean. "Le Mystere Pascal dans le Renouveau Liturgique." In *La Maison-Dieu* 67 (1961).

Gregory of Nyssa. *The Life of Moses.* Abraham J. Malherbe and Everett Ferguson, trans. New York: Paulist Press, 1978.

Habermas, Jurgen. *The Philosophical Discourse of Modernity.* Frederick G. Lawrence, trans. Cambridge: MIT Press, 1993.

Hatchett, Marion. *Commentary on the American Prayer Book.* New York: Seabury Press, 1980.

Hippolytus. *Apostolic Tradition.* Geoffrey J. Cuming, trans. Bramcote, Notts: Grove Books, 1976.

Horkheimer, Max, and Theodor Adorno. *Dialectic of Enlightenment.* John Cumming, trans. New York: Continuum Press, 1994.

Hughes, Graham. *Worship as Meaning: A Liturgical Theology for Late Modernity.* Cambridge: Cambridge Unviersity, 2003.

Irenaeus of Lyons. *Adversus haereses.* In *The Ante-Nicene Fathers.* Alexander Roberts and James Donaldson, trans. Grand Rapids: Eerdmans, reprinted 1987.

Jasper, R. C. D. and G. J. Cuming, eds. *Prayers of the Eucharist: Early and Reformed.* 3rd ed. New York: Pueblo Press, 1987.

Jungmann, Josef A., S.J. *The Early Liturgy: To the Time of Gregory the Great.* Notre Dame: University of Notre Dame Press, 1959.

Kavanagh, Aidan. *On Liturgical Theology.* New York: Pueblo Press, 1984.

Kilmartin, Edward J. "Theology as Theology of the Liturgy." In *Primary Sources of Liturgical Theology.* Dwight W. Vogel, ed. Collegeville: Liturgical Press, 2000.

Lathrop, Gordon W. *Holy Things: A Liturgical Theology*. Minneapolis: Fortress Press, 1993.

Lowe, Walter. *Theology and Difference: The Wound of Reason*. Bloomington: Indiana University Press, 1993.

Luther, Martin. *Martin Luther's Basic Theological Writings*. Timothy F. Lull, ed. Minneapolis: Fortress Press, 1989.

Lyotard, Jean-Francois. *The Postmodern Condition: A Report on Knowledge*. Geoff Bennington and Brian Masumi, trans. Minneapolis: University of Minnesota Press, 1984.

———. *The Differend: Phrases in Dispute*. George van den Abbeele, trans. Minneapolis: University of Minnesota Press, 1988.

———. *The Postmodern Explained*. Don Barry, et al., trans. Minneapolis: University of Minnesota Press, 1993.

Marion, Jean-Luc. *God Without Being*. Thomas A. Carlson, trans. Chicago: University of Chicago, 1991.

McIntyre, John. *The Shape of Soteriology*. Edinburgh: T & T Clark, 1992.

Mertens, Herman-Emile. *Not the Cross, But the Crucified: An Essay in Soteriology*. Gert Troch, trans. Louvain: Peeters Press, 1990.

Metz, Johannes Baptist. *The Emergent Church: The Future of Christianity in a Post-Bourgeois World*. Peter Mann, trans. New York: Crossroad Press, 1981.

———. *Faith in History and Society: Toward a Practical Fundamental Theology*. David Smith, trans. New York: Seabury Press, 1980.

———. "Freedom in Solidarity: The Rescue of Reason." In *Faith and the Future: Essays on Theology, Solidarity, and Modernity*. John Bowden, trans. Maryknoll: Orbis Books, 1995.

Milbank, John. *Theology and Social Theory: Beyond Secular Reason*. Oxford: Blackwell Publishers, 1990.

Mitchell, Leonel. *Praying Shapes Believing: A Theological Commentary on the Book of Common Prayer*. Minneapolis: Winston Press, 1985.

Morrill, Bruce T. *Anamnesis as Dangerous Memory: Political and Liturgical Theology in Dialogue*. Collegeville: Liturgical Press, 2000.

Norris, Richard. "The Result of the Loss of Baptismal Discipline." In *The Baptismal Mystery and the Catechumenate*. Michael W. Merriman, ed. New York: Church Hymnal Corporation, 1990.

Origen. "On Prayer." In *Alexandrian Christianity*. Henry Chadwick, ed. Philadelphia: Westminster Press, 1954.

Pickstock, Catherine. *After Writing: On the Liturgical Consummation of Philosophy*. Oxford: Blackwell, 1998.

Portalie, Eugene, S.J. *A Guide to the Thought of St. Augustine*. Chicago: Henry Regnery Company, 1960.

Power, David I. *The Eucharistic Mystery*. New York: Crossroad Press, 1994.

Ramshaw, Gail. "Pried Open by Prayer." In *Liturgy and the Moral Self: Humanity at Full Stretch before God*. E. Byron Anderson and Bruce T. Morrill, eds. Collegeville: Liturgical Press, 1998.

Saliers, Don E. *The Soul in Paraphrase: Prayer and the Religious Affections*. 2nd ed. Cleveland: OSL Publications, 1991.

Schmemann, Alexander. *Introduction to Liturgical Theology*. Crestwood: St. Vladimir's Press, 1986.

———. *The Eucharist*. Crestwood: St. Vladimir's Press, 1987.

Shepherd, Massey H., Jr. *The Paschal Liturgy and the Apocalypse*. Richmond: John Knox Press, 1960.

Sokolowski, Robert. *Eucharistic Presence: A Theology of Disclosure*. Washington, D.C.: Catholic University of America, 1994.

Steiner, George. *Real Presences*. Chicago: University of Chicago, 1989.

Stevenson, Kenneth. *Jerusalem Revisited: The Liturgical Meaning of Holy Week*. Washington, D.C.: Pastoral Press, 1998.

Stuhlman, Brian D. *A Good and Joyful Thing: The Evolution of the Eucharistic Prayer*. New York: Church Publishing, 2000.

Sykes, S. W. *Sacrifice and Redemption: Durham Essays in Theology*. Cambridge: Cambridge University Press, 1991.

Taft, Robert. "In the Bridegroom's Absense: The Paschal Triduum in the Byzantine Church." In *La Celebrazione del Triduo Pasquale: Anamnesis e Mimesis*. Rome: Ateneo S. Anselmo, 1990.

———. "What Does Liturgy Do? Toward a Soteriology of Liturgical Celebration: Some Theses." In *Primary Sources of Liturgical Theology*. Dwight W. Vogel, ed. Collegeville: Liturgical Press, 2000.

Talley, Thomas. *Origins of the Liturgical Year*. 2nd ed. Collegeville: Liturgical Press, 1991.

Tracy, David. *Plurality and Ambiguity: Hermeneutics, Religion, Hope*. Chicago: University of Chicago, 1987.

Turner, Victor. *The Forest of Symbols*. Ithaca: Cornell University Press, 1967.

———. *The Ritual Process: Structure and Anti-Structure*. Ithaca: Cornell University Press, 1969.

Tyrer, John W. *Historical Survey of Holy Week, Its Services and Ceremonial*. Alcuin Club 29. London: Milford Press, 1992.

Vogel, Dwight W. "Liturgical Theology: A Conceptual Geography." In *Primary Sources of Liturgical Theology*. Collegeville: Liturgical Press, 2000.

Von Balthasar, Hans Urs. *Mysterium Paschale*. 2nd ed. Edinburgh: T & T Clark Press, 1990.

———. *The Heart of the World*. Erasmo S. Leiva, trans. San Francisco: Ignatius Press, 1979.

Ward, Graham. *Cities of God*. London: Routledge Press, 2000.

Weaver, J. Denny. *The Nonviolent Atonement*. Grand Rapids: Eerdmans, 2001.

Williams, Rowan. "Does It Make Sense to Speak of a Pre-Nicene Orthodoxy?" In *The Making of Orthodoxy: Essays in Honour of Henry*

Chadwick. Rowan Williams, ed. Cambridge: Cambridge University Press, 1989.

————. *Eucharistic Sacrifice: The Roots of a Metaphor.* Bramcote, Notts: Grove Books, 1982.

Zimmerman, Joyce Ann. *Liturgy and Hermeneutics.* Collegeville: Liturgical Press, 1999.

INDEX